Egbert L. Viele

Hand-Book of Field Fortifications and Artillery

also manual for light and heavy artillery

Egbert L. Viele

Hand-Book of Field Fortifications and Artillery
also manual for light and heavy artillery

ISBN/EAN: 9783337270599

Printed in Europe, USA, Canada, Australia, Japan

Cover: Foto ©Andreas Hilbeck / pixelio.de

More available books at **www.hansebooks.com**

CHAPTER I.

FIELD FORTIFICATIONS.

FIELD WORKS are any constructions which have for their object to impede the advance of an enemy, or to enable an inferior force to maintain their position against the attack of a superior number.

The name of *field fortication* is applied to a work which is composed of an embankment of earth called a "parapet," and an excavation called a "ditch," on the exterior side which last furnishes the earth for the embankment.

The outline or form of the work varies with the character of the ground, the circumstances under which it is constructed, the strength of the force, and particular character of the defence. The profile or shape of the embankment or parapet is usually the same in all cases.

When the ground about a work within effective range of the firearms of the attacking party is quite flat, the height, called the "command" of the work, must be at least 7 feet 6 inches, in order that the defenders may be covered from the fire of men on horseback—that class of troops being able to discharge their arms at 7 feet 6 inches above the ground.

Unimportant works, or such as are situated on higher ground than that within effective artillery range, may have their parapets as low as 6 feet, or even 5 feet.

Fig. 1.—Plate 2 shows the ordinary form of the profile of an intrenchment, in soils of which the natural slope is one perpendicular to one base.

    A B C D E F is the profile of the Parapet.
    G H I K the profile of the Ditch.
    L M N the profile of the Glacis.
    A B the Banquette Slopes.
    B C Tread of the Banquette.
    C D the Interior Slope.
    D E the Superior Slope.
    E F the Exterior Slope.
    F G the Berm.
    G H the Scarp.

H I the Bottom of the Ditch.
I K the Counterscarp.
A the Foot of the Banquette Slope.
B the Crest of the Banquette.
C the Foot of the Interior Slope.
D the Interior Crest.
E the Exterior Crest.
F the Foot of the Exterior Slope.
G the Crest of the Scarp.
H the Foot of the Scarp.
I the Foot of the Counterscarp.
K the Crest of the Counterscarp.
M the Crest of the Glacis.
N the Foot of the Glacis.

Fig. 2 shows the general plan of intrenchments with flanking arrangements.

O A B and E F P are the Advanced Parts.
B C D E are the Retired Parts.
A O, A B, E F, and F P are the Faces.
B C and D E are the Flanks.
C D the Curtains.
A D and C F the Lines of Defence.
O A B and E F P are the Salient Angles.
B C D and C D E the Re-entering Angles.
A D F and B C F the Angles of Defence.
b A c and e F g the Sectors without Fire.
L M and N R the Capitals.

Sometimes the parapet* is formed of earth taken from an excavation or trench inside of it; in this case a parapet may be as low as 3 feet, because, then, the defenders standing in the trench of equal depth, and close behind the parapet, are sufficiently covered by it.

Should there be ground near the position to be fortified, higher than that on which the parapet stands, the latter must then have a greater command than 7 feet 6 inches, but in the more simple kind of field works the command does not exceed 12 feet; for as soldiers cannot easily throw earth with a shovel to a greater height than 6 feet, and as other means are generally wanting in the field, it is evident that the height of a parapet for such a work, must be limited by the capability of executing it with shovels and pickaxes by two parties of men, one standing on a level 6 feet above the other. The same reason determines the greatest depth of ditch to be 12 feet, a

---

* In this manner cover for troops may be very quickly obtained, with the advantage of having the power to advance over the parapet in order of battle when occasion offers.

scaffolding being necessary at 6 feet above the bottom of the ditch to receive the earth which is thrown from thence; the earth is then thrown up to the level of the ground, by other laborers placed on the scaffolding.

In the construction of field works it should always be recollected that a great command of parapet not only requires additional means, trouble, and time to throw up the earth, but also renders necessary an increased mass of earth for the banquette, which may thus encumber the interior of the work.

To obviate, as much as possible, the latter evil, it is usual to mount the banquette, by steps, when the parapet has a greater command than 8 feet.

The thickness of the parapets of field works must be regulated by the description of arms likely to be employed against them; in order, therefore, that they may afford a reasonable degree of resistance to repeated firing, the thickness of parapets must somewhat exceed the penetration of the shot which may be used in the attack.

Penetration of shot.	*Thickness of parapet.*
Musket ball, 10 to 18 inches.	3 feet.
6—pounder, 3½ to 4 feet.	6 feet.
9—pounder, 6¼ to 7 feet.	8 or 9 feet.
12—pounder, 8½ to 10 feet.	10 or 12 feet.

It is found by experiment that loose earth resists the penetration of shot just as well as that which has been rammed together.

Although a musket ball penetrates, at most, only 18 inches into earth, musketry parapets require to be made 3 feet thick, in order that they may be sufficiently substantial to preserve the requisite height, notwithstanding the action of the weather.

Heavier guns than 12-pounders are rarely brought into the field, consequently 12 feet may be considered as the greatest thickness of a parapet; and it has been shown that, for the simpler works, 12 feet is the greatest command of a parapet, and likewise the greatest depth of a ditch.

The exterior side of a parapet is formed with a slope which has a base equal to its height, that being the inclination which (ordinary) earth assumes when thrown up loosely; and, therefore, it is the most advantageous form for a mass of earth whose sides are unsupported.

The interior slope of a parapet has a base not greater than one-third or one-fourth of its height, in order to allow the men to approach near the crest, and to fire over the parapet with ease.

FIELD FORTIFICATIONS.

As newly moved earth will not remain at such a steep slope without support, it must be retained in that state by a revetment.

The REVETMENT is commonly made with gabions, fascines, sandbags, or sods of turf; or again with hurdles, casks, trunks of trees, and occasionally with doors, shutters, &c., from any neighboring houses. Trunks of trees are objectionable as a revetment for the interior slope, on account of the splinters that fly from them when struck by shot; and large trees, laid horizontally to revet the escarp or counterscarp, are defective, because they serve as steps for the assailants.

GABIONS are strong cylindrical baskets without top or bottom, 2 feet in diameter, and 2 feet 9 inches in height. These are placed in rows along the line of work at an inclination corresponding to the required slope, and then filled with earth. To make a gabion, from eight to fourteen pickets, 3 feet 6 inches long, are fixed upright in the ground, at equal distances, in the circumference of a circle, 1 foot 11 inches in diameter; flexible twigs (or rods) are then interwoven with the upright pickets, commencing with three rods at the bottom, and weaving each in succession outside of two pickets and inside of one; as the twigs (or rods) are expended, others are added, and the basket work continued to the height of 2 feet 9 inches; this work (which is called the web) is sewn in three or four parts, from top to bottom; withes, (called gads,) or spun-yarn being used for that purpose, in order to keep it from coming off the pickets; the ends of these are then cut off, about an inch from the web. A gabion, thus made, stands 3 feet high in the revetment, and weighs from 36 to 40 lbs. The best wood for the web, and particularly for the gads, is willow and hazel.

FASCINES are military faggots, 18 feet long and 9 inches in diameter: they can be sawed into shorter length, and are sometimes made only 6 feet long.

To make a fascine, two trestles (like a St. Andrew's cross) are fixed in the ground at 16 feet apart; then three or four other trestles (according to the length and thickness of the brushwood) are placed at equal distances between the two first trestles; and in a direct line with them; brushwood is next laid along the trestles, (the smallest inside,) so as to project 17 or 18 inches beyond the extreme trestles, and is compressed to a diameter of 9 inches by means of an instrument called a choker;* the brushwood is bound

---

* The choker consists of 4 feet of chain, with a wooden lever at each end. On the chain is marked, by rings a length of 28 inches, being a circumference equivalent, nearly, to a diameter of 9 inches.

with gads, (before the choker is relaxed,) at 6 inches beyond the extreme trestles, and at intermediate intervals of 15½ inches, and the ends of the fascine are sawed off square, at 1 foot beyond the extreme trestles.

FASCINE GADS are tough and flexible twigs, 5 feet long, very much twisted to render them fit for tying. A squad of five men can, in an hour, make a fascine which weighs (when tolerably dry material) from 140 to 160 lbs. If, however, the brushwood is green and much thicker than a man's thumb, it will weigh 200 lbs. The fascines forming a revetment are fastened in their position, (one above another,) by pickets 3½ or 4 feet long, which are driven obliquely downwards through the fascine so as to form an angle of 45° with the slope. The pickets should be in the proportion of 6 to an 18-inch fascine, of which two are driven vertically, in order to fasten each fascine to that which is beneath it.

Two gabions make nearly the same quantity of revetment as an 18-inch fascine, and consume but half the quantity of materials; moreover, they require only common laborers to form them into a revetment, and stand in their positions without pickets or other fastening; they also make a more durable revetment than fascines or sand-bags.

As fascines are heavy, require pickets to fasten them, and experienced men to build them in revetment; as, moreover, each fascine takes twice as much material as two gabions, which, together, will make a revetment of equal superfices, it is evident that fascines are inferior to gabions for the formation of revetments, although they support the earth at the same slope, viz., with a base equal to one-quarter of its height.

SAND-BAGS are bags of coarse canvas, measuring, when empty and laid flat, 2 feet 8 inches by 1 foot 4 inches; they contain, when quite full, a bushel of earth; but when tied and placed in revetment, only three-quarters of a bushel. In building a revetment with them they are arranged with their ends and sides presented alternately to the front in each course, and with the joints in the successive courses broken, like brickwork. Sixteen sand-bags build 10 square feet of revetment; they ought to be tarred, if the revetments are to last a considerable time; if not tarred, they rot in two months. An empty sand-bag weighs 1 lb. 2 oz., and when tarred 1 lb. 12 oz.

Filled sand-bags are musket-shot proof, and are frequently placed on a parapet, one across two others, the latter being a short distance asunder, in order that the intervals may serve as loopholes.

Gun batteries are sometimes made entirely of sand-bags, which are filled at a distance and brought to the place; this may be done either to save time, or when earth cannot be procured on the spot, in consequence of the soil being rocky or marshy.

On naval expeditions sand-bags are very serviceable, as there is no other way in which a battery can be promptly formed on a shore.

When sand-bags or gabions are made use of to revet the cheeks of embrasures, they should be covered with raw hides, to prevent them from being damaged by the flash and the concussion caused by the discharge of the gun.

SODS OR TURF, being generally procurable on the spot, are much used in the revetments of the slopes of field works; but there are strong objections to sod revetments, particularly as they take three times as long to build as a brick wall.

Good sods ought to be cut 16 inches long, 8 inches wide, and 4 inches thick; they are built up in the same manner as bricks, and with the grass downwards, and are fastened with pickets long enough to penetrate three courses. Six sods build 2 square feet of revetment. A sod revetment requires most labor; revetments of sand-bags, fascines, and gabions, require successively less; the last is the best in all respects; a sod revetment retains the earth at a slope of one-third only, the three others at a slope of one-fourth.

The parapet is bounded on its upper surface by a plane called the "superior slope;" this declines towards the counterscarp, in order to enable the defenders to see and fire on the assailants (directly) until they descend into the ditch. The amount of this slope is called the "plongée," and this varies from one-sixth to one-fourth of the thickness of the parapet, but it must not exceed one-fourth in order that the crest* of the parapet may not become too weak.

It is of great importance that the superior slope should be directed to the counterscarp, as it then enables the defenders, notwithstanding the smoke and confusion consequent on an attack, to direct their fire with certainty to a spot where the assailants' columns must be, more or less, detained by the ditch and the obstacles in it.

"If the superior slope cannot be directed to the edge of the coun-

---

* It has been found by experience that a soldier cannot depress his musket, when firing, more than 15° below a horizontal plane, and a plongée of one-fourth of the thickness of the parapet gives a depression of 15°; this is an additional reason for limiting the plongée to one-fourth of the thickness of the parapet.

terscarp without making the plongée more than one-fourth of the thickness of the parapet, the counterscarp must be raised by means of a small glacis. The crest of this glacis, however, should be kept at least 4 feet below the crest of the parapet of the work, that the assailants, when on the glacis, may not have the power of firing into the work.

The outer edge of the superior slope is called the "exterior crest," whilst the inner (and upper) edge of the same slope is called the "interior crest," or the "crest" of the parapet.

A step, called a "banquette," is placed at the foot of the interior slope, and from 4 feet 3 inches to 4 feet 6 inches below the crest, in order to enable the defenders to fire with ease over the parapet, and in the direction of its superior slope.

The terreplein, or tread of the banquette, is made 3 feet wide for one rank of men, and 4 feet wide if intended for two ranks. In order that the men on it may descend backwards with ease, there is a gentle* slope for that purpose, having a base equal to twice the height of the banquette.

The ditch is not excavated immediately at the foot of the exterior slope of the parapet, but at a distance from it, varying from 1 to 4 feet, according to the adhesiveness of the soil. This space of unmoved earth is called the berme, and it is requisite both to remove the pressure of the parapet from the immediate edge of the ditch, and to facilitate the construction and repair of the parapet. A berme has the defect of affording an intermediate landing-place on which the assailants may form; and although it may be occupied by obstacles, these require additional labor, and may be destroyed by cannon; yet a berme can scarcely be dispensed with unless the earth is very adhesive, and that the parapet is not more than 8 feet high.

The berme, in most cases, may be cut away after the parapet has had two or three days to settle.

The ditch will not be an effective obstacle if less than 6 feet in depth, and for the reason given, it is not made deeper than 12 feet.

The sides of the ditch being of unmoved earth, they will support themselves, without revetment, at a steeper slope than those of the parapet; and as the counterscarp has not the weight of the parapet to resist, and is not exposed to fire, it may, generally, be made steeper than the escarp.

---

* If the parapet has a greater command than 8 feet, this convenience is relinquished on account of the great space occupied by it, and the banquette is ascended by steps.

The slopes of both vary from a base equal to the height to a base of one-quarter of the height.

To find the breadth of the ditch, (of the usual shape,) divide the area of a profile of the parapet by the intended* depth of the ditch, and the quotient is the mean breadth of the latter; to this, add half the sum of the bases of the escarp and counterscarp slopes for the breadth at top, and deduct the same half sum for the breadth at bottom.

The best shape for an unflanked ditch is one having a triangular section, as it does not permit the assailants to form at the bottom; and moreover, with an equal depth and area of section, it may be made wider at top than a trapezoid would be; by which means the superior slope of the parapet can be directed to the counterscarp without too much increasing the plongée, or without raising the counterscarp by a glacis.

To find the breadth of a ditch having a triangular section, divide the area of a profile of the parapet by half the given depth of ditch, and the quotient is the required breadth at top; the sides may evidently have any given inclinations to the horizon consistently with the given breadth, depth, and area of a transverse section.

THE OUTLINES OF FIELD WORKS.

The direction which a parapet is made to assume in order to enclose, or partially enclose, the ground to be fortified, is called the outline of a work.

The following are general principles to be observed in determining the outlines of field works:

1st. There should be a reciprocal defence between all the parts of works, so that the ground over which an enemy must pass to the attack should, if possible, be seen both in front and in flank.

2dly. The "lines of defence" must not exceed the effective range of muskets, viz.: about 160 yards.

3dly. Re-entering† angles (viz.: flanking angles,) ought never to be less than 90° and seldom more than 100°; for, if less than 90°, the men on the flanking parts would fire against each other; and if more than 100°, the fire of the flanking parts would diverge too far from the salient to be flanked.

---

* This is determined chiefly by the nature of the soil and the size of the parapet.

† In both these cases it is presumed that the soldier fires (as he generally does) at right angles to the parapet behind which he stands.

Redan, Cremaillere, Line and Star Forts

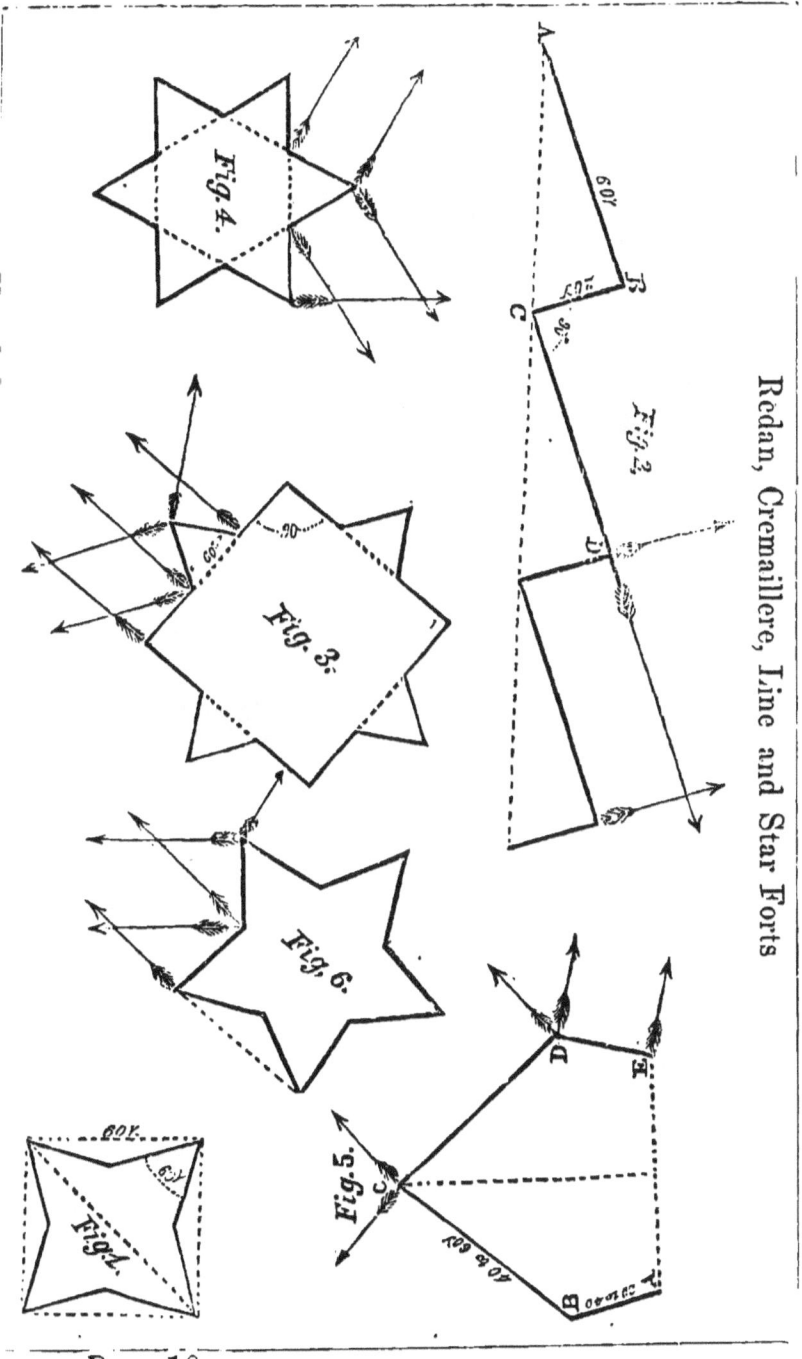

4thly. The salient angles of works should be as obtuse as possible, and never less than 60°, otherwise the interior space might become too contracted; the angle would be so sharp as to be quickly worn away by the weather, and would be easily battered down; also the* undefended sectoral space in front of the salient angle (which is the supplement of the angel) would become very great; and

5thly. The outline of a field work should be proportioned in length to the number of men and guns intended for its defence. One man occupies a space of three feet.

The names of the works most commonly employed in field fortification are redans, single, double, and triple; redans with auxiliary flanks; lunettes, redoubts, star forts, bastioned and demi-bastioned forts, block-houses, and works used mostly for lines of intrenchment, such as tenailles and crémaillères.

The REDAN is a work consisting of two faces, which form with each other a salient angle, the rear being open. When the faces are not more than about 20 yards in length, the work is sometimes called a fléche.

The redan is in the most advantageous position when the ground before the salient angle, and approaches to the gorge, are inaccessible, or when the work can be supported by troops; for example, when, with obstacles in its front, it is employed as an advanced work to defend hollow ground which cannot be seen from the principal work—to protect a bridge, a dam, a road, a defile, or to cover a guard, an advanced post, &c.

The weak points of this work are: that it has an open gorge, and that its ditch, and the ground in front of the salient angle, are undefended either by direct or flanking fire.

On account of its having an open gorge, it is seldom advisable to construct a redan as an isolated work; its rear should be exposed to the fire of some collateral work, or have free communication with a body of troops in its rear, to whom it may form an advanced post, or outwork; or otherwise the faces should terminate on a river, a marsh, or any inaccessible ground, which would prevent it from being turned.

The first defect, viz.: that of having an open gorge, may be remedied in a slight degree by placing along the gorge abatis, trous de

---

* Undefended by direct fire. To prevent the enemy from approaching the work on these undefended sectors the salients should be directed towards some natural obstacle, such as a marsh, &c.; or if this cannot be done, then artificial obstacles should be disposed in their front.

loup, &c., (or palisades, if time and materials abound;) as for the second defect, a direct fire may be brought in front of the salient either by rounding the latter, or by cutting off the angle by a short face not less than 6 yards long.

A flanking fire may be procured for the ditch and salients, by forming auxiliary flanks, which may be placed either towards the middle or at the extremities of the faces; such a flank ought not to be less than than 12 yards long, that there may be, at least, 12 men firing from it.

DOUBLE REDANS consist of two redans joined together, their exterior faces being generally longer than the others: the French call a work of this kind a queue d' hyronde.

A TRIPLE REDAN consists of three redans joined together, the exterior faces of these are also, in general, longer than the others.

A LUNETTE is a large redan with flanks parallel or nearly parallel to the capital; as a general rule, the flanks are traced perpendicularly to the intended line of fire, for the purpose of bringing on certain spots a more direct fire than could be made from the faces of the work.

It is often desirable to secure the gorges of these works against surprise; this may be done by disposing across the gorge a single or double row of palisades, or a stockade-work, in the form of a front fortification or of a tenaille: there should be a banquette to it, that the defenders may have a command over the assailants, and a ditch to prevent the enemy from getting close, and cutting, burning, or blowing down the obstacle. Trous de loup, abatis, and chevaux-de-frise are sometimes disposed across the gorge for the same purpose.

A REDOUBT is a closed work, the parapet of which does not form re-entering angles; it may be quadrilateral, polygonal, or circular.

Circular redoubts, although they have no undefended sectors, and enclose a greater space than any other redoubt with an equal length of parapet, are seldom formed on account of the difficulty of their construction, and also because their ditches are incapable of any flanking defence; the lines of fire diverging from the parapet, any one spot on the ground is very imperfectly defended.

A four-sided figure is the best and most usual form for a redoubt, because it is of simple construction; the ditches are more easily flanked, and there are not so many points of attack as in a redoubt of a greater number of angles. Redoubts, being closed works, are better calculated to stand detached than redans or lunettes, and are, therefore, constructed when a small work is required without any immediate protection from the gorge—the armed party being strong enough to complete and man a four-sided redoubt, each side of which is not less than 15 yards long.

The size depends on the number of men who are to garrison it, and upon the number of guns which it is to contain; also upon the length of time during which it is to be occupied: this may be for a few hours only, (as on a field of battle,) or for a period of weeks or months.

If wanted only for a few hours, it will be sufficient to allow 3 feet in length of parapet for every man of the detachment; or for every two men, if they are to be formed in double rank. If guns are to be placed in the work, 15 feet of parapet must be given to each, in order that the gunners may have sufficient room on each side to work it.

But when the redoubt is destined to contain a body of men for a considerable length of time, it becomes necessary to have room for them to lie down within the banquette with their arms and packs; supposing one-third to be on guard, patrolling, &c., two square yards, in addition to the slope of the banquette, are sufficient for each man, and 36 square yards for each gun with its appointments.

The rule, consequently, for a square redoubt is: to multiply the given number of men by 2, and number of guns by 36, for the number of square yards which the work ought to contain within the foot of its banquette; the square root of the product will be the length in yards of the side of the square forming that area; adding to this result the breadth of two interior slopes, and of 2 banquettes with their slopes, (about 7 yards altogether,) we shall have the side of the square formed by the crest of the parapet.

A square redoubt ought not to be traced with less extent of side than 15 yards; for, by employing the calculation explained above, it will be found that such a work is only just sufficient to contain the men necessary for its defence: on the other hand, it is unusual to make a square redoubt with a longer side than 40 yards, because it would require a garrison more suitable to a work of a stronger outline.

The imperfections of redoubts are, that they are entirely without a flanking fire for the defence of the ground in front of their faces, also that their ditches and the sectoral spaces before the angles are without any fire whatever for their defence.

A flanking defence for the ditches may be obtained by placing palisade or stockade caponnières in them, either at the angles or in the middle of the faces; by tambours in a like position, or by loop-holed galleries under the counterscarp at the salients of the work.

The want of a fire in the directions of the capitals may be remedied, as in the redan, by cutting off an angle by a short face, by making it curved, or by tracing a portion of the line of parapet *en crémaillère;* viz.: by disposing it in a succession of salient and re-entering angles, the sides of which are alternately parallel to the capital: this construction is, however, very difficult, and causes inconvenient variations in the thickness and height of the parapet.

A ditch caponnière is an oblong structure formed with palisades, or with stockade work, loop-holed, and roofed over with planks and earth to secure the men from the effects of shell, and a plunging fire from the counterscarp. It ought, if possible, to be flanked with musketry, to prevent an enemy from closing on it, and getting under cover.

The best position for a caponnière in the ditch of a redoubt is at the salient angle, as then one caponnière flanks two branches of the ditch. It should be separated from the counterscarp by an enlargement of the ditch, to prevent an enemy from using it as a bridge to cross the ditch, and it ought to have a wicket to allow of sallies into the ditch.

The bottom or sole of the caponnière may, sometimes with advantage, be sunk 3 or 4 feet below the bottom of the ditch, in order that the fire from the loopholes may graze along it, and prevent an enemy from closing on them; by this construction; and by making the roof convex, it becomes more difficult for him to use the caponnière as a bridge to pass the ditch.

To lessen the destructive effect of shell, traverses should be placed in all closed works when those missiles are likely to be employed against them.

From the interior to the exterior of closed works there must be a passage through the parapet, protected by a traverse or by stockade work, and the traverse should extend far enough on each side of the passage to intercept shot which might enter it obliquely. The ditch is crossed by a bridge which is conveniently formed of loose planks and beams, because, in case of attack, they can be quickly taken up and used to barricade the passage. When the ditch is more than twelve feet wide, a trestle must be placed in the middle to support the beams or sleepers.

When rough timber only can be procured, stout straight limbs of trees must be selected for the sleepers, which may be covered with strong hurdles, (or brushwood,) over which a layer of sods and then a small quantity of gravel may be laid.

A STAR FORT is a closed work. the parapet of which forms several acute salient angles and obtuse re-entering angles, giving it a form like the usual representation of a star.

It has been seen that redoubts are defended only by direct fire, and that without some contrivance for affording flanking fire, the sectors at the salients, as well as the ditches, are absolutely undefended. Star forts, consisting of re-entering as well as salient angles, are intended to obviate that defect in some degree. They may be constructed either upon an exterior or interior polygon. If ground is to be fortified which does not admit the possibility of working outwards, as an island for instance, a polygon is traced to suit the form of the ground; the sides of the polygon are bisected by perpendiculars drawn inwards, and the faces of the star fort are drawn from the angles of the polygon to the inner extremities of the perpendiculars: this is called fortifying upon the exterior polygon.

The length of the perpendicular* in a square, pentagon, hexagon, and octagon, should be respectively one-eighth, one-fifth, one-fourth, and one-third of the side, in order that the flanking angles may approach as near as possible to right angles, without making the salient angles less than 60°. When the polygon is irregular, the length of the perpendiculars must be determined by the angles nearest to them.

Again, it may be required to surround a building with a star fort in such a position that the work could not be traced inwards; then, a polygon surrounding the building must be laid down, and on each of its sides an equilateral triangle must be formed towards the exterior.

If this construction be applied to a dodecagon, it will be found that the re-entering angles are exactly right angles; in an octagonal fort the re-entering or flanking angles are each equal to 105°.

The necessity for employing a polygon superior to an octagon will rarely occur; yet with irregular figures it may happen that some of the angles, are equal, or nearly so, to those of regular polygons of more than twelve sides.

It is necessary to fix some limit as a minimum to the length of face for these works; this depends on the distance at which a shot fired from the parapet of a face would reach the level of the ground; for it is evident that if the face be made less than that dis-

---

* The lengths given are merely approximations in the form of the nearest simple fraction of the side.

tance, the enemy, arrived at the rounding of the counterscarp, will be more or less secure from the fire of the adjoining face. If we suppose a man to fire along the superior slope of a parapet with a plongée of one-sixth, and that the work has a command of seven and a half feet, we have by similar triangles,

$$1 : 6 :: 7\tfrac{1}{2} \text{ (the command)} : 45;$$

the distance, in feet, at which the shot would reach the level of the ground.

The face should, therefore, not be less than 45 feet, viz., 15 yards. If the bottom of the ditch on any face is to be defended by the fire of the next face, a still greater length is required: to find this, we have the proportion 1 : 6 :: the relief (the height of the crest of the parapet above the bottom of the ditch) : the distance at which a shot would reach the bottom of the ditch; this distance is 30 yards when the command of the work and depth of its ditch are both seven and a half feet. The length of the faces depends also upon the number of guns to be placed behind the parapet, and upon the strength of the garrison; but 35 yards may be considered as the greatest length of face, for the troops required to defend a star fort having a longer face would be sufficient to construct and defend a fort of a better tracing.

The construction of star forts is attended with some trouble, particularly if the ground is uneven: such works present at their acute salient angels numerous points of attack: the faces and salients are without flanking defence when the polygon is inferior to an octagon, and even in this case such defence is imperfect; the ditches are undefended, unless the faces are made unreasonably long; the line of parapet to be manned is very great, when compared with the interior space, and is exposed to be enfiladed in all directions.

CONSTRUCTIONS.

The following are convenient methods of tracing on the ground the most useful polygonal redoubts and star forts:

For a pentagonal redoubt: on a base equal to one-fifth of the perimeter, or length of the parapet, form an isosceles triangle, of which each of the equal sides is one-third of the perimeter, and on each side of this triangle as a base form another isosceles triangle with its (equal) side, each equal to the side of the pentagon, or first base.

For a hexagonal redoubt: trace an equilateral triangle, the side of which is in length three times that of the redoubt; trisect each side, and join the nearest outer extremities of the centre portions: these lines, with those which join their extremities, will constitute the hexagonal redoubt required.

For a hexagonal star fort: trace an equilateral triangle on a base equal to one-fourth of the whole length of the parapet; trisect each side, and form equilateral triangles on the three centre portions. These will complete the figure.

For an octagonal redoubt: trace a square on a side equal to three-tenths of the whole length of parapet of the redoubt; and from the angles of the square measure on each side half the diagonal; the points being joined, the magistral line is traced.

For an octagonal star fort: trace a square on a base equal to three-twentieths of the whole length of the parapet of the star fort; with this square form an octagon as before, and on each of its sides trace an equilateral triangle.

FORTS WITH BASTIONS are the most perfect of closed field works, as it is evident that they possess all the advantages of mutual defence afforded by the corresponding works in permanent fortifications; they are traced similarly to these last, although rarely on a polygon superior to a pentagon; as, however, their defence mainly depends on the fire of common muskets, their lines of defence must not exceed the effective range of such arms, or about 160 yards, and therefore the side of the polygon on which they are constructed must not exceed 200 yards in length.

On the other hand, the side of the polygon should not be less than 120 yards in length; since, if it were so, the bastions would be too small, and the flanks and curtain too short for the defence required from them.

Bastioned forts should have within them a good reduit, in order to give confidence to the garrison, and secure its retreat: such a reduit should have a command of four or five feet over every part of the main work, in order that the enemy, having gained the parapet of the latter, may not fire from thence into the reduit.

The reduit may either conform to the outline of the fort, or it may be a simple redoubt, a blockhouse, or a tower of brick or stone, so traced that the defenders may fire into the bastions of the fort, these being the points at which an enemy is most likely to force an entrance.

As bastioned forts require a strong garrison, they are constructed when it is intended to occupy a point of importance for a considerable time, and, therefore, the reduit often forms, at the same time, the barrack of the garrison.

In order to throw an additional fire towards the direction of the salients, the curtain is sometimes broken in the prolongation of the lines of defence; but in order that some fire may be directed immediately in front, a portion may be formed in a line parallel to the original curtain, and equal to about one-third of its length; the two brisures should form with each other a re-entering rather than a salient angle, in order that there may be no dead spaces in the ditch.

The counterscarp of the ditch may be drawn either to the shoulder angles of the bastions, as in permanent fortification, or parallel to the faces, flanks, and curtain; the latter method is generally preferable, as it saves time and labor; in this case, however, the counterscarp of one flank would conceal the ditch of the nearest face from the fire of the opposite flank; this counterscarp ought, therefore, in part, to be cut away in an inclined plane, or ramp, parallel to, or coinciding with, the line of fire from that flank.

DEMI-BASTIONED FORTS, like those with bastions, are traced by letting fall a perpendicular from the middle of each exterior side, and drawing lines of defence; but each front has only one flank, every alternate face extending from the angle of the polygon to the inner extremity of that flank, and coinciding with the line of defence throughout its entire length; such works have the defect of affording a regular flanking defence only to every alternate face; as the short face of each front receives a very oblique and imperfect flanking defence from the collateral long face.

LOOPHOLES are narrow rectangular openings made in walls of masonry or wood, through which to direct a fire of musketry. In walls of two feet or two and a half feet thick they are about nine inches high by fifteen inches wide on the inside, and twenty inches high by four inches wide on the outside. In timber six or eight inches thick they are eight inches wide inside and three inches outside, the height being twelve inches.

They are made wider on the inside than on the outside, because, thus formed, they afford better cover for the men behind them; they are placed at not less than three feet asunder, that the wall may not be too much weakened, and that the men firing through them may not be crowded; they are made from four feet to four and a quarter feet above the banquette or ground on which the men stand to fire through them.

STOCKADE WORK is a wall composed of trunks of trees, or rough pieces of timber placed upright in the ground; they are made to touch each other, and loopholes are cut through them; if composed of trees, they ought to be squared, that the parts in contact may be of the same thickness as the rest of the wall.

A TAMBOUR is an enclosure of palisades or stockade work, sometimes with a ditch and banquette, and of any form that may be necessary to afford the defence required.

BLOCKHOUSES are covered field works, generally rectangular; the walls are formed of trunks of trees, and above the timbers of the roof there is, usually, a bed of earth, three or four feet thick.

In mountainous and well-wooded countries blockhouses are the best description of field works, because the enemy cannot easily bring cannon to destroy them. It is very difficult in mountainous countries to find ground where works may be constructed free from the defect of being commanded, and consequently open works are there comparatively useless.

Blockhouses are of great advantage as reduits in situations where it is difficult to defilade the interiors of works from commanding heights, more especially since they may serve as barracks for the troops; in such a case the bedsteads, arranged on each side, are used as banquettes, and the loopholes are made four feet above them.

A blockhouse to resist musketry should be composed of trees, squared so that the parts in contact may be at least six inches thick, that being the depth to which a musket ball will penetrate in fir. In order to resist artillery, two rows of trees (or of stockades) are placed vertically in the ground, with an interval between them from three to six feet wide, which is filled with earth well rammed. The trees or logs should be eleven or twelve feet long, so that they may be planted at least three feet in the ground, and allow the interior of the blockhouse to be eight or nine feet high; it should also be from eighteen to twenty-four feet wide in the interior.

The earth used to render the covering shell-proof may be shaped like a small parapet, and from this an additional fire (of musketry) may be obtained; the access to this upper parapet is through a trap-door in the roof. To prevent the blockhouse from being set on fire, a ditch should be dug round it, leaving a berme of eight or ten feet, and on this the earth is piled up against the wood as high as the loopholes.

Sometimes blockhouses are constructed in the form of a cross, when the flanking fire thus obtained on their faces renders them much more powerful; they are also, occasionally, built with an upper story, the angles of which should project over the sides of the lower story; the foot of the lower walls may thus be defended by the fire from above.

An ordinary dwelling-house, with thick masonry walls, may be formed into a blockhouse by pulling down the upper stories, and heaping a mass of materials, three or four feet in thickness, over the ceiling of the lower rooms; earth or rubbish should also be placed about the house as high as the loopholes.

DEFILADING OF FIELD WORKS.

To DEFILADE a work from a height is so to regulate the direction and elevation of the parapets or covering masses, that its interior may be screened from the view of an enemy on the heights.

A PLANE OF SIGHT is an imaginary plane supposed to pass through the summit of the height from which the work is to be defiladed, and the terreplein of the work.

A PLANE OF DEFILADE is a plane supposed to pass through the crest of the parapet of the work parallel to the plane of sight.

In many situations it is practicable (and then it is the easier method) to defilade the faces or longest branches of a work by the tracing; viz., by directing them on marshes, rivers, lakes, precipices, hollows, &c., where batteries cannot be erected, or at worst, on points of the height not nearer than 800* yards to the work. Also the choice of the outline of the work should be attended to; for among the different tracings by which the same object may be attained, some will be more easy to defilade than others.

When a work is thrown up in front of a height, it is the more difficult to defilade in proportion to its depth; it should, therefore, have an oblong form, and its longest faces should be traced parallel to the hieght. If, for instance, the work were a rectangular redoubt, the long faces should be traced parallel to the height, and the short ones be directed on it.

An open work will be defiladed when the plane of defilement passes through a line 8 feet above the ground at its gorge, and at a

---

* Artillery on a height, even of 120 feet, at 800 yards distance from a work, has no more advantage, in respect of a plunging fire, than if it were on a level with the rock; for in both cases it must be elevated about $1\frac{1}{4}$ degree to attain this range.

point 4 or 8* feet above the commanding hill, according as the work is to be defiladed against artillery or musketry.

It is usual to defilade a work against musketry if there are heights within 300 yards of it, and against artillery, when the heights are not farther distant than 800 yards.

When the commanding ground is not occupied by the enemy, the work may be defiladed in the following manner: stretch a rope between two poles planted in the line of the gorge at 8 feet above the ground; direct visual rays from various points of this rope to the top of a pole placed on the commanding hill, and 4 feet high if the work is to be defiladed against artillery, but 8 feet if it is to be defiladed against musketry; the intersection of the rays with poles planted on the tracing of the intended parapet, will indicate the height to which the parapet must be raised in order that its defenders may be situated under the plane of defilade; and since these visual rays represent lines of fire from the enemy's position on the hill, it will be evident that a parapet whose height is thus determined will defilade the interior of the work.

When it is impossible to place the pole on the commanding ground, the following method must be adopted: along the gorge of the intended work stretch a rope, which is to be 4 feet above the ground if the work is to be defiladed against artillery, and 1½ feet if against musketry; in rear of this rope at any convenient distance (about 5 yards) drive two pickets into the ground, and upon them raise or lower a cord or a straight edge of wood, until it is in the same plane with the rope at the gorge, and the top of the height from which the work is to be defiladed; then look from the rear cord or straight edge along that at the gorge, and observe where the line of sight from thence cuts the poles raised on the tracing of the intended parapet; these points of section (indicating the position of the plane of sight) may be marked by one of the party; lastly, make the crest of the parapet 4 feet higher than the points thus found if the work is to be defiladed against cannon, but 6½ feet higher if against musketry.

If it is found that, by this process, the parapet must have more than 12 feet command in order to defilade the work; the parapet must be raised to any convenient height, (suppose 10 or 12 feet,) and then, in order to defilade the part which is not protected by

---

* A field-gun stands about 3½ feet above the ground, and a man on horseback can fire about 7½ feet above the ground; therefore 4 and 8 are taken as the nearest whole numbers to these commands respectively.

the parapet, a traverse must be erected, or the terreplein of the unprotected part must be lowered, or both of these steps must be taken conjointly.

In defilading a téte de pont, the plane of defilade should pass 8 feet above that part of the bridge which is most remote from the height.

To defilade a closed work, (or one with a parapet both on the side nearest to and on the side furthest from the height,) unless the crests on both sides are in a plane passing 8 feet above the ground which the enemy may occupy, in front and in rear, a parados to cover the defenders on the banquette of the side nearest to the height from reverse fire, is indispensable; for it is clear that the higher the parapet nearest to a commanding ground is raised in order to defilade a portion of the whole of the interior of the work, the more will the defenders standing on the banquette of that parapet be elevated above the plane of defilement of the parapet furthest from the height, (or the lower one;) they will, consequently, become exposed to a reverse fire directed over the lower parapet.

In this case, therefore, make the parapet nearest to the commanding ground as high as convenient, and so as to defilade a portion (suppose one-half) of the interior: at the extremity of this defiladed portion, and (about) parallel to the parapet, raise a parados high enough to intercept visual rays directed from points 8 feet above the banquette of the lower parapet to 4 or 8 feet above the height, and from points 8 feet above the banquette of the higher parapet to points 8 feet above the ground in front of the former parapet.

If the site of the intended redoubt be commanded on opposite sides, the work will be defiladed in the manner just described, excepting that, in this case, both the parapets being commanded, each must be raised high enough to cover the portion of the work between it and the traverse or parados from the opposite height.

Or the work may be defiladed thus: the magistral line having been traced, let the engineer place himself at any convenient part of the interior with his eye 8 feet from the ground, and let a man hold up a measuring rod on the tracing line between the engineer and each hill; then a visual ray, from a point estimated to be 8 feet above each hill, will intersect the measuring rods in points through which the crests of the parapets should pass. The place of the engineer is the place of the traverse or parados, the height of which is determined, as before, by visual rays crossing each other from points 4 or 8 feet above the opposite heights to points 8 feet above the banquettes most distant from the heights.

With the aid of a plane table, the plane of sight may be readily determined thus: let the upper surface of the table (which should be near the surface of the ground in rear of the work) be placed in a plane touching the points of command: the intersections of that surface prolonged, with the poles planted at the angles of the work, will determine as many points in the plane of site.

PROFILING.

The proper height of parapet for the work having been determined, (by the process of defilading, if necessary,) the next step is to plant pickets on the faces, flanks, and angles as guides to the workmen in giving it the suitable dimensions and form. Thus, to the magistral line of each face and flank, trace on the ground perpendicularly at intervals, and on these measure, horizontally, the bases of the slopes composing the profile to be employed. At the points thus set out * fix poles or laths perpendicularly in the ground, and saw off their tops at the height which the parapet is to have at that particular part; nail laths to the tops of these poles from one to the other across the direction of the intended parapet; and thus there will be obtained an outline of the slopes, or a profile of the parapet.

For the profile at an angle, lay a rope on the ground bisecting that angle, and produce it outwards; drive pickets along this rope at the points where it is intersected by the prolongations of lines joining the bases of the profiles already set up perpendicularly to the adjoining faces; these pickets mark the bases of the profiles at the salient; the laths may then be set up as before.

When the salient angle is 60°, the breadth of the base of any slope measured on the capital will be equal to twice the breadth of the same slope taken on a line at right angles to the face.

DISTRIBUTION OF THE WORKING PARTY.

Divide the men into 6 equal parts, 3 of which are to be provided with pickaxes and shovels, 2 are to have shovels only, and the remainder are to be furnished with rammers only.

The party is then to be marched to the ground, and the men,

---

* The best method of fixing the perpendicular laths is to drive strong pickets into the ground at the required points, and to nail to them the laths, previously cut of the proper length.

having both pickaxes and shovels, (viz. the diggers,) are to be stationed 6 * feet apart on the ground where the ditch is to be dug along the berme line, and facing the work.

The excavation of the ditch is now begun, the men first loosening the earth with their pickaxes, and then shovelling it to the place where the parapet is to stand; here the rest of the party are posted, and as the earth is thrown up to them, the men with shovels spread it in layers, while the remainder with their rammers, beat it down to a firm mass; and as the parapet is raised they give it the form indicated by the profiles.

The profiles may be made of 3 inch plank, ripped up into laths three-quarters of an inch thick.

The work may be drained, if requisite, with fascines of stout rods, or with loose stones having brushwood or heather laid over them; these are placed in trenches dug across the ground on which the parapet is to be raised.

In excavating ditches and trenches, the slopes are made after the ditch or trench is finished, the sides being at first left in steps; the crest of the slope is marked out, and then small sections are cut, here and there, according to the proper form of the finished profile: finally, the intermediate earth is cut away between these small sections; the latter answering the purpose of ensuring regularity in the excavation of the ditch, as the lath profiles ensure it in the erection of the parapet.

When near the surface, in soil requiring but little the use of the pickaxe, an excavation of 6 cubic yards in a day of 8 hours would be a fair task for a soldier, who, in general, is little accustomed to the use of the pickaxe and shovel.

In calculating the time required to throw up a field work, the following data may be assumed; in light, dry sandy soil, that can be easily dug without the aid of a pickaxe, a man can, in a day of 8 hours, load from 19 to 20 cubic yards of earth on barrows. If a pickaxe be required, two men can do the same quantity of work.

If the whole mass must be first moved with the pickaxe, three or four men should be allowed.

A man can wheel 20 cubic yards of earth per day to a distance of 30 yards on level ground, or 20 yards on a ramp.

Twenty cubic yards of earth will fill 500 wheelbarrows.

---

* The diggers must not be placed nearer to each other than $4\frac{1}{2}$ feet; but if the party is strong, another row of diggers may be employed at the counterscarp, with their backs to the work; these throw the earth towards the middle of the space marked out for the breadth of the ditch.

A horse can do as much work as 7 men: he can carry 300 lbs. 20 miles per day, or 200 lbs. 30 miles; he can draw 1,600 lbs. on a plain, and from 1,200 to 1,300 lbs. on irregular ground, when the roads are in good order.

OBSTACLES.

Palisades are triangular prisms of wood pointed at the upper end, and placed upright in the ground at 3 or 4 inches asunder; they are about 10 feet long, with faces 6 or 8 inches wide, and are sunk 3 or 4 feet in the ground. A trench of that depth is dug, the palisades are placed in it, and the earth is well rammed about them; they are connected at top (and sometimes at bottom also) by a ribbon of wood, called a lintel, 4 inches wide by $2\frac{1}{2}$ thick, nailed to the inside of the palisades about one foot from the points; they ought to stand, at least, 7 feet out of the ground. Rough palisades may be formed, quickly, from trees by cutting them into lengths about 10 feet, then describing triangles, with sides of not less than 6 inches in length on the ends, and sawing them lengthwise through those sides; if the trees are 12 or 14 inches in diameter, six equilateral triangles meeting in the centre, can be described on the ends, and six palisades made of one piece: if the tree is but 6 inches in diameter, then, by sawing it in halves, two palisades can be made of one piece.

Palisades are only used in the ditches, and to close the gorges of field works, and are not, as in permanent works, placed on the banquettes; when in the ditch, their best position is at the foot of the counterscarp, and slightly inclined towards it; for, thus placed, they are more secure from a direct fire of artillery, and they detain the enemy at the counterscarp under the deadly aim of the garrison; also it makes it difficult for the assailants to cut them down, there being no room between them and the counterscarp to stand and wield the axe.

Fraises are palisades about 11 feet long, placed in a horizontal or in an inclined position; they ought to be sunk about 5 feet in the ground, the buried ends being joined by a ribbon in order to render it difficult to pull them out; the pointed ends ought to be not less than 7 feet from the bottom of the ditch; and when placed on the berme they ought to incline downwards, in order that they may not interrupt the passage of shells when rolled over the parapet. Fraises are most advantageously placed 2 or 3 feet below the edge of the counterscarp, as they are, there, more secure than on the berme, from the direct fire of the enemy, whom they detain under a close fire from the work.

Chevaux-de-frise are beams of wood from 6 to 10 feet long, which are cut in a square or hexagonal form, and have pointed stakes or sword blades inserted into the faces; when several are used, in one length, they are chained together to prevent the enemy from removing them; and they are made of the lengths just mentioned in order that they may be portable.

They are employed as temporary barriers to impede the passage of a breach, the entrance into a work, to block up a street. &c.; they are occasionally placed at the foot of the counterscarp of the ditch, and, also, on the berme; in the latter situation they must be covered from the view and fire of the enemy by a small glacis.

Abatis are large boughs or entire trees laid down in a line, with the butt ends buried 3 or 4 feet in the ground, and the branches turned towards the enemy: to form an efficient obstacle, the branches ought to stand, at least, as high as a man's breast, the smaller parts being cut off, and the larger pointed; the butts should be secured in the ground by beams or trees picketed across them, and they should be covered with earth well rammed; this precaution will make it difficult to drag them away. They ought, moreover, to be covered by a glacis, that they may not be seen and breached or destroyed at a distance, by artillery.

A detachment of 90 men can make about 750 feet of abatis in a day.

Some of the trees on the borders of a wood being formed into abatis, may deter an enemy from attempting to penetrate into the wood. A breastwork may be made of trunks of trees piled one on another to the required height behind the abatis; this is soon done, and it much increases the strength of the obstacles.

Trous de loup are holes dug in the ground in the form of an inverted cone or pyramid, and are made about 6 feet wide and 6 deep: a pointed stake is planted at the bottom to prevent an enemy from making use of them as rifle pits. In order to form an effective obstacle, they should be disposed checker-wise in three rows, with intervals of about 10 feet between them; the earth from them should be formed into a glacis, rather than heaped up between them, as in the latter case they might be easily filled up.

Trous de loup of even two or three feet deep, may be usefully employed in rendering impassable shallow wet ditches, inundations, and fords; and, as well as abatis, they are suitable obstacles to the advance of an enemy on the salients of works, on the weak points of lines, or through their intervals; they may thus compel the enemy to attack the stronger parts.

The gorges of works may also be closed by abatis and trous de loup, when there are no means of planting palisades for that purpose.

A man can make one trou de loup in a day.

An *Entanglement* is formed by cutting half through the stems of small trees, and pulling the upper parts to the ground, to which they are then picketed.

Crows feet are four iron spikes joined together at one end in such a manner, that when thrown on the ground one point will always be uppermost; they may be quickly made by inserting four spikenails into a small block of wood, so as to point in different directions; they are chiefly employed to obstruct the advance of cavalry.

Pointed Stakes are frequently fixed in the ground, at any place which the enemy might occupy at the time of an assault; as on the bermes of works, the edges of trous de loup, and in the spaces between them. They must be firmly planted in the ground, and if they are pointed before insertion, two mallets must be used, one of which is provided with a conical hole to receive the point of the stake, while the blows are struck with the other; these pickets may be conveniently formed of the small branches cut from the trees intended for abatis.

Common Fougasses are small mines placed in shafts or pits from 3 to 10 feet deep.

The powder is lodged on one side of the shaft at the bottom, and is fired from a secure spot by means of a powder hose, or fuse, which is brought up one side of the shaft, and carried in a trough (or casing tube) parallel to the surface of the ground; the trough should be 5 or 6 feet below the ground if there is any danger of shells falling on it; if not, 2 feet will be deep enough.

A *shell fougass* is formed by dividing a box into two parts by a horizontal partition; the shells being loaded, are placed in the upper part, with the fuzes pointing down through holes in the partition in order that they may be ignited, at the same moment, by the priming; the latter consists of a few pounds of powder placed in the lower compartment.

Shell fougasses are very convenient obstacles to impede the passage of a ditch and the ascent of a breach, as they can be prepared within the work, and speedily buried at the required spot just before their action is required.

A stone fougass or *rock mortar* is thus formed. Excavate a shaft at an inclination of about 45° to the horizon, and about 6 feet deep; at the bottom place a charge of 55 lbs. of powder, then a strong shield of wood (at least 6 inches thick) in front of the charge; and over the shield throw in 3 or 4 cubic yards of pebbles of not less than half a pound weight each; a sufficient body of earth must be heaped vertically above the charge, and retained over the upper part of the shaft (near the edge) by a revetment of sods, to ensure its effect taking place in the direction required.

Twelve men can make a stone fougass in three hours, which, being charged as before described, will, when exploded, disperse the materials over a circle of 30 or 40 yards radius, at about 60 yards from the mouth of the shaft.

The usual and most effective position for fougasses is beyond the ditch and over the salients or other weak points of the work; they must be removed in advance of the ditch so far as not to injure the counterscarp by their explosion.

A good method of discharging fougasses at the moment required, is to place a loaded musket with the muzzle in the priming and a wire attached to the trigger; the wire can be led in any direction, in the same manner as the hose, and being pulled at the proper moment, the explosion will take place.

INUNDATIONS.

It frequently occurs in the field that small streams or rivulets are met with, which of themselves offer no impediment to the advance of the enemy, but which, by judicious management, may be made effectually to check his attack on certain points where the water may be collected.

An inundation, or collection of water, is produced by forming across a stream one or more dams, which must extend to a certain distance from thence, according to the inclination (or slope) of the ground contiguous to the stream, and to the required breadth of the inundation.

A dam may be formed in the following manner: after constructing an embankment of earth on each side of the stream perpendicularly to its length, as far as the bank, stones and gravel should be thrown into the water to diminish its depth; then two heaps of earth are prepared, one on each bank, and as many workmen being set on as can be employed without impeding each other, the earth from those heaps is thrown into the stream over the stones and gravel as rapidly as possible, until the embankments previously formed are connected together across the stream.

It rarely occurs that sufficient means are to be found in the field to allow of a dam being made more than ten feet high; and supposing this height to be given, the difference of level between any two dams should be five feet, in order that the shallowest part of the inundation may be five feet deep, and therefore, not fordable.

The distance at which the dams should be placed from one another will depend upon the fall of the bed of the stream, and must be determined by levelling. The thickness of the dam at top may be made equal to the depth of the water intended to be retained, but if it is liable to be battered by artillery, it should be ten feet thick at top. The exterior slope of the dam may be left at the natural slope of the earth, while to that opposed to the stream a base of not less than double its height should be given.

A sluice or waste weir should be provided at the height to which it is desired the water should rise; otherwise, the water being allowed to flow over every part, the dam would be destroyed. These openings, or waste weirs, must be revetted with fascines or timber, and ought to be completed before the dam is carried up to its full height.

Sometimes the inclination of the ground contiguous to the stream prevents the inundation from attaining a depth greater than two or three feet; it may, notwithstanding, be rendered impassable, by digging pits and ditches in different parts before the water is allowed to cover the ground.

The end of the dam on the enemy's side must be protected by field works to prevent him from destroying it, or using it as a bridge. When no work can be placed immediately to cover the head of the dam, the approaches to it should be defended; or if the opposite bank be within short musket range, the end of the dam may be covered by abatis. The works thrown up to cover the head of a dam are traced precisely on the same principles as those which are to protect a bridge. The best condition, therefore, when a choice is possible, is, that the inundations should be concave to the enemy.

Small islands may exist in the midst of an inundation, and on these batteries or breastworks for musketry may be advantageously formed, either to protect the dams, or for the general defence of the position.

TETES DE PONT.

Têtes de pont are works thrown up to cover a communication across a river, to hinder the destruction of the bridge, and to defend it until an army or detachment has crossed over it.

They should be of sufficient strength to be defended until the whole of the troops have crossed and the bridge has been taken up. The works employed for this purpose vary according to the nature of the ground to be occupied, the shape and width of the river, the importance of the communication, &c.: they consist of redans, lunettes, hornworks, or portions of any kind of field work.

If the bridge is seen from any point on the bank, the tête de pont should have at least one face, whose fire may sweep that point.—Islands should be made to contribute to the defence by works erected on them; these should be breastworks for infantry, if the work is within the range of that arm, or batteries for field guns. Advantage should also be taken of the opposite bank to fortifiy it in a similar manner. If these measures cannot be taken, auxiliary flanks may be added to the faces of such a work as a redan for the defence of the salients.

A reduit is frequently constructed within a tête de pont, to cover the bridge from the neighboring heights, and also to enable a small party of the troops to keep the enemy in check until the main body has crossed, and the bridge has been taken up; this rear guard then crosses the river in boats or rafts, protected by the fire from the opposite side.

A battery should be constructed so as to enfilade the bridge, and to destroy it, should the enemy force the reduit.

The faces or flanks of a tête de pont should have such directions given to them that their fire may range directly along the banks.

The best position for a (temporary) military bridge and tête is at a re-entering bend of a river; viz., at a part which is concave towards the enemy's side, because then the bank which is in possession of the force about to lay down the bridge, in part, envelope both that and the tête. Thus, while the bridge is covered from the view of the enemy, breastworks or batteries may be advantageously placed to assist in its defence, and at the same time to give an effective cross fire in its front.

When, however, the bridge is to remain a considerable time, these advantages must be given up, and a straight part of the river chosen, because there the current acts directly against the heads of the boats or pontoons, whereas at a bend it acts obliquely against the sides, and thus tends constantly to derange their positions. Again, at a bend the current is constantly wearing away the concave side, (or bank,) and depositing the earth thus removed at the next convex bend, thus causing a shallow bank to be formed on one side of the river and a deep part at the opposite side; consequently at every fall of the water, in such a place, one end of the bridge is left aground on the shallow part, while the other end descends with the water, and thus the bridge is in danger of being broken.

It is evident that the bed of a river will be less irregular, and that fords will be most usually found where the course is straight; fords are, however, occasionally found at the bends of a river in directions obliquely across, from one convex part to the next on the opposite side.

A ford should not be more than four feet deep for cavalry, three feet for infantry, and two feet four inches for artillery.

LINES.

Lines are a series of works and trenches, or of independent works, arranged so as to defend each other, and the ground in front of and between them.

Lines are used to cover the front of a position, or to connect important redoubts or forts together.

Lines are of two kinds, such as are continuous, and such as have intervals between the works.

The former are principally applicable to situations where it is proposed to act on the defensive only, and where they are of such limited extent that the whole line of parapet can be occupied with troops exclusive of the reserves; as, for instance, to close a pass between scarped mountains, or on the sea shore, or on the banks of large rivers; thus resting on natural obstacles, which will prevent their flanks being turned. They are often introduced as portions of an extended line with intervals.

Extensive continued lines can make but slight resistance, while the labor necessarily expended in executing them is considerable; and as the enemy may menace several points at once, it follows that nearly as many troops would be required for the defence as are employed in the attack, in which case the first principle of fortification is violated. Even if the defenders have a sufficient number of disposable troops, they act, when within lines, under a disadvantage, for they must watch and follow every movement of the eneny, so as to be equally prepared to resist a false and a real attack. It has often happened that while the defenders within lines were concentrating their forces to oppose a false attack, the enemy has penetrated at a point where he was not expected; and a continued line once entered may generally be deemed lost.

Continuous lines of redans connected by curtains are constructed in three ways: in the first, as described by Vauban, the salients of the redans are at 240 yards asunder, and consequently the musketry fire of one redan does not, effectively, defend the salient of the next. To remedy this defect, it was subsequently recommended that the salients of the redans should be brought within musket range of each other, or within 160 yards.

In both of these constructions the flanking angles formed by the faces of the redans and the curtains joining them much exceed 105°, and consequently the flanking defence is very imperfect.

In the third construction the salients are removed to 240 yards from each other, (the original distance,) but the curtain is broken into two parts, forming a salient angle, and thus the re-entering or flanking angles are reduced to but little more than 90°, by which means the flanking defence is greatly improved.

This tracing is, however, still defective, inasmuch as it presents double the number of salients to the enemy's attacks, and the branches of the broken curtains are exposed to be enfiladed, which is not the case in Vauban's construction.

Lines of tenailles consist of parapets forming a series of salient and re-entering angles, and are, in fact, like the improved redan lines, except that, in this tracing, the redans are all of the same size, and have obtuse angles.

They are traced by setting off distances of about 200 yards along the front of the intended lines, to mark the position of the salient angles; these intervals are then bisected, and perpendiculars drawn towards the interior to give the places of the re-entering angles. The perpendiculars should not exceed half the distance between the salients, otherwise the re-entering angles would be less than right angles.

Crémaillère lines are composed of alternate short and long faces at right angles (or nearly so) to each other; the short faces, called crotchets, are made about 30 yards long, and the long faces, called branches, about 100 yards long.

These lines possess the following advantages:

1st. The branches are but little exposed to be enfiladed, owing to the small projection of the salients.

2dly. Each branch is defended not only by the fire of the adjoining crotchet, but by several others.

3dly. Their outline is very easily adapted to all varieties of of ground; and on slopes, in particular, they are very advantageous, because a small additional height given to the crotchets will defilade a long extent of branch from the fire of an enemy on the height.

Their defects are:

1st. The crotchets being short, very little of the ditch of each is defended by the adjacent branch.

2dly. A battery which can enfilade one branch is equally able to enfilade several.

Crémaillère lines may be much strengthened by placing along their front bastions or double redans, at intervals varying from 690 to 800 yards, in order that a cross fire of artillery may be brought from them in front of the other parts of the line.

The crotchets should face towards the bastions, or redans, in order that the fire from the crotchets may defend the salients of those works, and that the branches may be defiladed by being directed on the bastions or double redans. When the line crosses a valley, the branches may be most effectually defiladed by giving the whole a bend concave towards the exterior, and placing the bastions, or redans, on the high ground; these works will thus form the more advanced parts of the line.

The flanks of the bastions must be connected with the next crotchets on both sides by broken curtains, taking care that the re-entering angles are not less than right angles.

Bastioned lines are made precisely in the manner already pointed out for the fronts of bastioned forts; such lines may be strengthened by lunettes, constructed at musket-shot distances in their front, and having their faces directed upon those of the bastions, in order that the ditches of the lunettes, and the ground in front of them, may be defended by those faces.

The flanks of the lunettes give a direct and close fire in front of the salients of the bastions; but care must be taken in their construction that they do not fire into each other; on this account, when the fronts are in one straight line, it is usual either to suppress the flanks of the lunettes, or to place a lunette on every alternate front only.

The communication from the lines to the gorge of each lunette is by a caponniére, which is, generally, made broadest at the inner end, in order, to enable the garrison to meet the enemy on a superior front, should he succeed in getting into it; its parapet is made only 3 feet above the ground that it may not mask the fire of the lines, and consequently its interior must be sunk 4 or 5 feet to afford the requisite cover; its breadth must be sufficient to allow room for a banquette. A traverse is placed at its inner extremity, and perhaps, (according to the nature of the ground and the length of the passage,) at intervals along the passage.

Sometimes the line changes its direction; in such cases, when the change causes the parts of the line to form with each other a re-entering angle, the latter is one of the strongest parts of the line.

LINES WITH INTERVALS, OR BROKEN LINES.

Broken lines should always, when practicable, be disposed in a double row, and in such a manner that the inner works may flank the outer; the advantages possessed by broken lines are:

1st. With the same extent as continuous lines, they require less labor in the construction, and fewer troops to occupy them, consequently large reserves may be formed.

2dly. The defenders may advance in force and in a regular formation through the intervals, and attack the enemy, should he have been thrown into confusion.

3dly. They oblige the enemy to overpower each separate work before he can become possessed of the whole; whereas if a continuous line be forced in one part, it is generally lost to the defenders.

4thly. If the enemy has gained one work he will then be exposed to the flanking fire of the adjacent works, and to a fire from the works in the second line.

To profit fully by this advantage, when the front line consists of closed works, their rear faces ought to be of slight construction, that the artillery of the second line may easily demolish those faces, if the enemy should gain possession of the works.

When there are two lines of works, the heaviest artillery should be placed in the inner line, or else the enemy, obtaining possession of the exterior line, would turn the guns against the other, and have a superiority over the defenders.

When lines are on sloping ground descending towards the front, the slope should, if possible, be cut very steep, so as to form an escarpment before the works.

A single row of redans or redoubts is comparatively weak, for the fire from them crosses at a distance in front of the intervals, and but feebly defends the salients. Lunettes are better in such a situation on account of the fire of the flanks, which may be brought to cross the capitals close to the salient angles.

The intervals between the works which form a broken line should not exceed 160 yards, in order that they may be defended by an effective cross fire from those works.

The different works should occupy the most prominent and the highest ground; also the flanking parts ought to be perpendicular to their lines of defence.

The intervals between the works may be strengthened by artificial obstacles, or by a trench, for troops, with a rough parapet, (like the first parallel in a siege,) having a broad interior slope to enable the men to advance over it when occasion requires.

DEFENCE OF FIELD WORKS.

A spot selected for a military post should not be commanded, especially on the flank or in the rear, within the ordinary range of a field piece. There should be plenty of materials on the spot to aid in strengthening the works, or in forming obstructions in front of them. The soil should be of a nature to be easily worked, and the position should be difficult of access; it should, however, offer the means of retreating in security, and with facility.

The highest ground of a position should be occupied by the salients of works, for then the adjoining faces will be, in some measure, secured from enfilade fire; it follows that the re-entering angles should be placed in the lowest spots.

It is very essential to create obstructions within short range of musketry in front of all works of a temporary nature, with a view of breaking the order of the assailants, and detaining them under a close and severe fire, if they persist in forcing their way through.

In fact, all the movements of an enemy, whether to the front, to the right or left, should be a much cramped and impeded as possible; it is important to break his order and put him into confusion when under fire, for he can seldom re-form under such circumstance; and if he attacks in disorder, the chances are against his success.

To save time in making palisades or stockade work, the whole quantity ought to be divided into distinct portions, say 10 or 12 feet in length, to one carpenter and two laborers; and to prevent confusion in obtaining materials for constructing obstacles, it is well to divide the men into parties of 8 or 10 each, prescribing to each party the nature of the materials, required, the place where they are to be obtained, and the spot at which they are to be deposited.

The materials are obtained by felling trees, unroofing houses, taking up floors, and the like.

The guns of a work should not, generally, reply to the cannonade which precedes an assault, but should be placed behind traverses, or other places of shelter previously prepared for them; they should only fire at the enemy's artillery, while the latter is changing its position.

Round shot or shells are fired against guns; grape, canister, spherical case, and rockets against troops.

As soon as the enemy's light troops advance, the parapets are to be manned; sand-bags previously filled are placed along the parapet, leaving loopholes between them; they are musket-shot proof, and give the men the necessary confidence to enable them to take a steady aim. One rank of men is sufficient on the banquette, others being placed behind them to load. A reserve is to be stationed under cover, who fall upon the assailants with the bayonet, should they succeed in getting into the work. For a good defence there ought to be a file per yard to man the parapet, with a reserve of one-fourth or one-sixth of the whole, in addition.

As soon as the assaulting columns begin to mask the fire of their own artillery, the guns of the work will be brought up, and open their fire on them.

A sortie (very rarely) may be made, should the enemy be thrown into disorder; but this step requires great caution, for should the sortie be repelled, the enemy may enter the work with the retiring troops.

Fougasses, having been previously prepared, will be fired the instant the enemy is above them, by means of a piece of safety fuze, or a musket with its muzzle in the powder and a wire to the trigger.

If the assailants at length descend into the ditch, shells, grenades, and every sort of missile are to be thrown upon them. The shells are rolled down by being placed in troughs laid on the superior slope of the parapet.

If the enemy has to cross a river before he arrives at the work, the fords may be rendered impassable for artillery and cavalry, by digging pits, planting stakes, throwing in felled trees and harrows, or by driving wagons or carts full of stones into the middle, and taking off the wheels.

Should the ford be beyond musket range from the work, a parapet may be raised opposite to it, at such a distance from it as to permit the defenders to issue forth and charge the party crossing it, at the moment they land in disorder on the bank.

To prevent surprise, outposts are stationed round the work at night, and heaps of dried brushwood, or tarred fascines, should be placed along the post at intervals; at the approach of the enemy, the outposts retire into the work, having set fire to the piles of brushwood; this will, in a great measure, prevent an enemy from concealing himself near the work.

LOOPHOLING WALLS.

Walls are made available for the purposes of defence by loopholing them; if a ditch cannot, for want of time, be dug at the foot of the wall outside, the loopholes ought to be, at least, 7 feet above the ground to prevent the assailants from making use of them; in the former case a temporary stage might be made of casks, ladders, &c., within 4 feet or 4 feet 6 inches of the loopholes, to enable the men to fire through them.

The quickest way of loopholing a wall is to break it down from the top in the form of narrow fissures about 3 feet asunder; but if the wall is very low, or there is not time to make loopholes, a piece of timber, or the trunk of a tree, supported on the top of it by a couple of stones, would be a ready expedient, and men could fire from the opening under it; or sand-bags, or large stones or sods, might be placed on the wall at intervals. The loopholes made in walls or buildings can seldom be of any regular form; the width outside should not exceed 3 inches, but inside it may be equal to the thickness of the wall. The best tools (of such as are usually found about building) to break loopholes through a wall, are crowbars, pickaxes, and large hammers.

Barricades for roads and streets are made, if time permits, by sinking a ditch 7 or 8 feet deep, and forming the earth into a breastwork, adding palisades, &c.; but, if time presses, casks, boxes, or cart bodies filled with earth, stones, manure or cinders, sacks of flour, bales of merchandise, and the like, must be arranged across; paving stones may be taken up and disposed in a similar manner.

The mass should be raised 6 or 7 feet high, and a banquette formed for firing over it; the neighboring houses should also be loopholed so as to give a good flanking fire over the ground in front of the barricade, and stones may be collected to throw down on the assailants from the contiguous houses.

FORTIFYING HOUSES.

The great art of converting buildings, and the outhouses and walls that usually surround them, into defensible posts, consists in selecting from the mass of objects at hand such as will answer the purpose, and in sacrificing every thing else; making use of the materials to strengthen the part which is to be fortified.

The building chosen should possess some of, or all the following requisites.

1st. It should command all that surrounds it.

2dly. It should be substantial, (not thatched,) and of a nature to furnish materials useful for placing it in a state of defence.

3dly. It should be of an extent not too great for the number of the defenders, and should only require for the completion of the proposed object the time and means which can be spared.

4thly. It should have projections flanking the walls and angles.

5thly. It should be difficult of access on the side exposed to attack, and yet have a safe retreat for the defenders; and, of course, it must be in such a position as to answer the purpose for which the detachment is posted.

As a rough guide to judge of the third requisite, there ought to be a man for every 4 feet of wall round the interior of the lower story, one man to 6 feet for the second story, one to 8 feet for an attic, with a reserve of about one-sixth of the whole.

Should there exist any doubt about having sufficient time to execute all that might be wished, it would be necessary to decide on the best points to be secured, in order to repel an immediate attack; in such a case it might be well to employ as many men as could work without hindering each other by being too crowded, to collect materials, and barricade the doors and windows on the ground floor, to make loopholes in them, and to level any obstruction outside that would give cover to the enemy, or facilitate the attack; to sink ditches opposite the doors on the outside, and arrange loopholes in the windows of the upper story; to make loopholes through the walls generally, attending first to the most exposed parts, and to break communications through all the party walls and partitions; to place abatis or any feasible obstruction on the outside, and to improve the defence of the post by the construction of tambours; to place outbuildings and garden walls in a state of defence, and establish communications between them; to make arrangements (in the lower story particularly) for defending one room after another, so that a partial possession only could be obtained on a sudden attack being made.

These different works should be undertaken in the order of their relative importance, according to circumstances; and after securing the immediate object for which they were designed, they might remain to be improved on, if an opportunity should offer.

Houses are fortified by piercing loopholes through the walls, and if the walls are high, two, or even three rows of loopholes may be made, and a temporary scaffolding of furniture, casks, &c., erected for firing from the upper ones: one row may be made close to the ground, with pits dug in the rear, or the floor may be cut through, if there is a basement, for the convenience of making use of them. The loopholes may have the dimensions before prescribed, and they ought not to be made at a less distance than three feet from each other, lest the wall should be too much weakened, or the defenders inconveniently crowded.

The staircases are to be cut away, the communication being kept up by ladders; and the floors, as well as the partition walls, should be loopholed.

Thatched roofs and all combustible materials are to be removed, and barrels of water should be placed in every room in readiness to extinguish fire.

A communication ought to be opened on the side furthest from the enemy, through which ammunition and reinforcements may enter.

The door or barrier closing this communication may be made musket-proof by nailing strong planks to it, and if there is a basement to the house, the floor should be cut away within the door, so as to form a sort of ditch.

All the doors and windows are to be barricaded and loopholed. The best barricade for a door is made by strong palisades, which are secured to a thick cross beam let into the wall on each side; a bank of earth may also be formed on the exterior.

A flanking defence can always be obtained by constructing a tambour in front of a side, or at the angles of a house.

All enclosures which may afford the enemy cover must be removed, if not included in the defence.

If artillery is likely to be employed against the house, it will be necessary, unless the walls are very strong, to support the timbers of the roof by means of props.

If there is time, the house may be formed into a blockhouse by pulling down the upper stories, and laying the materials over the lower rooms to make the covering shell-proof.

A ditch may be dug on the outside of the house, and the earth placed against the walls: some protection may be obtained for the doors, by placing strong beams against the walls on the outside in an inclined position, and heaping earth or rubbish over them.

INTRENCHING A VILLAGE.

In intrenching a village, the buildings, walls, and hedges on its circuit are to be considered as part of its enclosure, and are to be made fit for the purposes of defence; all the intervals between them are to be occupied by breastworks or palisades, and strengthened by abatis.

The streets are to be barricaded at intervals with carts or wagons having one or two wheels taken off, with barrels of earth, bales of merchandize, &c. A passage should be made through the adjoining houses, which should be loopholed, and care must be taken that the barricade be not turned by an enemy passing down the neighboring streets.

Some strong building, such as a church, court-house, or jail, should be selected, and fortified with particular care, to serve as a citadel or reduit, to which the defenders may retire when driven in from the exterior part of the village.

Advantage must be taken of any walls or outbuildings surrounding whatever has been selected as the reduit or keep; and they should be converted into outworks for strengthening it as an independent post. Should the village be of too great an extent for the force thrown into it, a portion of it only might be strengthened, and the remainder separated or destroyed; or the defence might be confined to some separate building.

The roads by which an enemy would advance should be cut up, and obstructed with felled trees, ploughs, harrows, &c.; bridges should be broken, and the passage disputed under cover of some simple field work placed favorably to command the road.

The resolute defence of villages situated on the front of an army has often decided the fate of a battle; in this position, they may be regarded as bastions connected by movable curtains.

ATTACK ON FIELD WORKS.

The attack on field works may be executed by surprise, or by open force; the former can only take place when the advance of the assailants is concealed by fog or darkness, or by the nature of the ground, as in mountainous countries.

In the attack of field works by open force, it is advisable to advance against several points at the same moment, when circumstances permit; of these some may be false attacks, and may be converted into real ones if the enemy appears weak or hesitating on the points threatened. One attack ought, generally, to be directed upon the rear of the work, (if open at the gorge,) which will always lessen the confidence of the defenders.

As many assaulting columns should be formed as there are points to be attacked, and before the works are stormed, pits and trenches should (when time permits, and there is no natural cover for skirmishers) be dug to conceal riflemen: these pits are about four feet wide, and, with the excavated earth raised before them, four feet in depth, in order that they may serve to cover a file of men to that height.

The artillery should be posted on the prolongations of the faces to enfilade them, weaken the parapets, and ruin the interior defences of the work and its ditch; for the latter purpose howitzers are best adapted. As soon as the artillery has produced some effect, the signal for the assault should be given; light troops will gradually advance towards the counterscarp, in skirmishing order, firing at the gunners through the embrasures; they will conceal themselves in the pits and trenches prepared for them, or seek shelter in the inequalities of the ground. They should be followed by storming parties, and these should be accompanied by a detachment of sappers, (or a squad of soldiers told off for that purpose,) carrying axes, crowbars, bags of powder, &c., to force obstacles. Lastly, the reserve will follow, at some distance, to act as circumstances may require; it may repel attempts to aid the defenders, reinforce the storming parties if they succeed in entering the work, or it may afford them a rallying point, and cover their retreat if they fail.

The troops descend into the ditch with unfixed bayonets, in order to avoid accidents; and they fix them when on the berme.

Should the ditches have a great depth, it will be necessary to lessen it by means of bags with heather or grass, or by bundles of hay or straw, or fascines, &c.

A bridge formed of a gun limber and a ladder may be run up to the counterscarp and thrown across.

To avoid mistakes in marching by night to attack, each soldier should bear some visible mark by which he may be distinguished from an enemy. If a breach or any particular point is to be attacked by night, the way to it should be marked by distinguishable pickets or other objects, placed or re-marked on the ground at the time of the previous reconnoissance.

The columns march to the assault in the direction of the capitals; but after passing the ditch, the troops should enter the works by the faces, on each side of the salient angle, that they may present a front in the work equal or superior to that of the enemy. When it may be advisable to force an entrance at the gate of a fortified post, that gate may be destroyed by a piece of artillery brought close up to it, or by a bag of powder attached to the wood by a gimlet, or propped against it by a forked stick.

In assaulting a place whose scarps and counterscarps are revetted with masonry, scaling ladders must be employed. The first division of each column of assault carries the longest ladders; they descend into the ditch with them, and afterwards carry the ladders across and raise them against the scarp.

The next division carries other ladders, which they place and leave against the counterscarp. The ladders are carried and planted with arms slung. Ladders planted against a wall are not to slope above one-fourth of their height, lest they should break under the weight of the men.

A strong firing party is drawn up on the glacis to keep down the fire of the defenders, if the latter should appear on the parapets to oppose the assault.

ATTACKING HOUSES.

In the attack of houses, artillery should be employed to form a breach before giving the assault, and also to throw hot shot, shells, and carcasses.

If the detachment is unprovided with artillery, attempts must be made to force passages through doors, windows, or unflanked parts of the walls: the attack should be made on different parts of the building, to distract the attention of the defenders; in the mean time, and for the same purpose, parties of men keep up a fire on any points where there is a chance of disabling them. Attempts may also be made to effect an entrance through the roof, by means of ladders.

If the assailants have neither powder nor crowbars for forcing doors, a heavy beam or tree may, if at hand, be used as a battering ram; a fire of straw or brushwood may be made near the walls further to distract and alarm the defenders, and to cover the operations of the assailants.

ATTACKING BARRICADES.

Artillery will soon clear a passage through ordinary barricades; if not, the assaulting party must endeavor to turn the barricade, either by passing down some other street, or by forcing a passage from one house to another, until they arrive in rear of it: a few loaded muskets applied to the locks and bolts of the strongest door will force it open, and the partition walls may be destroyed by bags of powder, &c. After having taken possession of a house, troops must be left in it for the purpose of firing from it upon the barricade.

CHAPTER II.

ARTILLERY.

The pieces of artillery in ordinary use are: guns, howitzers, and mortars. They are made either either of iron or brass, (gun metal.)

Brass guns are made of a metal composed of 8 parts of tin to 100 of copper, and cost about $900 per ton; iron guns cost $100 per ton.

Brass guns are used for field batteries, as they can be made with a less quantity of metal than iron guns of the same calibre, without danger of bursting. Therefore, though brass is heavier than iron, guns of the former metal are lighter than those of the latter. Brass guns, are however soon rendered unserviceable by repeated and quick firing.

Iron guns are better adapted for the attack or defence of fortresses, and for service on board of ship, being less expensive than those of brass, and better able to sustain long continued and rapid firing.

At the siege of St. Sebastian, each piece fired 350 rounds in $15\frac{1}{2}$ hours without becoming unserviceable: brass guns could not have fired 120 rounds in the same time, without drooping at the muzzle and running at the vent so much as to become useless.

The length of a gun is measured from rear of the base or breech-ring to the face of the muzzle.

The CALIBRE is the diameter of the bore.

The DISPART is the excess of half the diameter of the base ring (or thickest part of the gun) above half the diameter of the muzzle. Guns are made thicker at the breech than at the muzzle, the better to resist the expansive force of the powder.

The TRUNNIONS are projections or arms one on each side of the gun, by which it is secured and supported in the carriage.

The WINDAGE is the excess of the diameter of the bore over the diameter of the shot, and is, in field guns, about 1-40 the diameter of the shot; in iron guns it is about 1-6 inch*.

Guns are named according to the number of pounds contained in the round shot they carry; thus a 6-pounder carries a 6 lb. shot; a 12-pounder carries a 12 lb. shot, etc.

The service charge of powder for battering is one-third of the weight of the shot.

The charge for field guns is from 1-6 to 1-4 of the weight of the shot, as a greater charge is found to injure the carriages without producing an equivalent effect.

For ricochet firing, the charge varies from 1-18 to 1-36 the weight of the shot; and the elevation of the gun from 5° to 9°.

To increase the range of the gun, an increase of elevation above a horizontal line must be given to the axis of the gun.

In pointing a gun, the line of direction is given from the trail, and the elevation from the breech.

Point-blank position of the gun denotes that the piece is laid, directly, at the object without elevation: to effect this, the lowest notch on the side of the base ring, the notch on the side of the muzzle, and the object to be fired at, are brought into one line; the two notches are in a plane passing through the axis of the bore, and that plane may be parallel or oblique to the horizon.

Point-blank range is the distance from the muzzle of the gun to the first point at which the shot strikes the ground; it being supposed that the latter is parallel to the axis of the bore.

If the gun is pointed at an object, by looking along the upper surface of it, (for which purpose there is a notch behind the vent, and one on the top of the muzzle,) it is said to be laid by the line of metal, and it gives the gun an elevation of about one degree; the breech being wider than the muzzle.

The upper right hand quadrant of the base ring has 12 quarter degrees (called quarter sights) notched on it; by bringing the object, the notch on the side of the muzzle, and any quarter sight into one line, a corresponding elevation or depression is given to the gun.

The tangent-scale is raised from a groove behind the vent, and can be fixed at any point of its length by a screw; it is divided into quarter degrees from one degree upwards: by means of this scale

* 12, 9, and 6-pounders have 1-10 inch windage; a 3-pounder has 9-100 inch; 32-pounder from 1-5 inch to 1-8 inch, according to the length; 24-pounder about 1-6 inch; 18-pounder about 1-7 inch. Carronades have a windage of 1-64 the diameter of the shot.

the requisite elevation, as far as 6 or 8 degrees, may be given with great accuracy, the object being seen in a line with the top of the tangent-scale, and the notch on the top of the muzzle.

The point-blank range of light (brass) 12, 6, and 3-pounders, is 200 yards; medium 12 and 9-pounders, and heavy 6-pounders, 300 yards; iron (long) 24-pounders, 360 yards.

Every quarter of a degree of elevation increases the range of each class by 100 yards until there are attained, respectively, the ranges of 600, 700, and 1200 yards, after which each quarter of a degree increases the range by a less amount than 100 yards.

Howitzers* are a short description of ordnance with chambers, and are used, principally, for projecting shells horizontally or nearly so.

Their principal advantages are, that they can be more easily loaded, and are considerably lighter, in proportion to the calibre than guns; they may, also, be used as mortars: they have no dispart, the diameter of the base ring and swell of the muzzle being equal, or the difference being made up by a patch on the muzzle.

Howitzers are intended for enfilade and ricochet firing, to reach troops behind heights and parapets, and to breach earthen works by firing shell into them: for these purposes heavy charges are not necessary, although the bores may be large; the chamber is formed so as to confine the powder as much as possible, and so that the shell may rest on its mouth.

Mortars differ from guns in the construction of their bore, their chamber being in the shape of a frustum of a cone, by which means the powder is confined, and the shell fits close to the sides; they are also much shorter and thicker than guns: they have trunnions at the extremity of the breach, and are usually placed on their beds so as to project shells, carcasses, or fire balls at an angle of 45°, the range being increased by augmenting the charge of powder.

The shells discharged from mortars describe a high curve in their flight, and fall with their full weight almost vertically upon the object to be struck; they thus fracture the strongest buildings, and bursting at the same time, they set fire to every thing combustible about them.

Their splinters are also very destructive, and fly in all directions, sometimes as far as 400 yards. As mortars fire over the parapet,

---

*The charges for certain howitzers are as follows:—10-inch, 7 lbs.; 8 inch, 4 lbs.; 5½-inch, (24-pounder,) 2 to 2½ lbs.; 4 2-5 inch, (12½-pounder,) ¼ to ½ lb.

and not through embrasures, it is necessary that they should be placed at a distance of 12 feet behind the crest of the parapet, supposing it to be of the ordinary height.

Rockets are cylindrical cases of pasteboard* or iron, attached to one end of a rod of wood, and containing a composition, which being ignited, they are projected through the air by a force arising from the combustion.

Military rockets terminate either in a cone or a parabolid, and may serve either as shells or carcasses: their weight is from 3 to 32 ℔. They are, in general, fired from tubes, and the proper elevation is about a degree for each hundred yards in the intended range. Fired against troops they create much disorder, and falling on buildings, they destroy them or set them on fire.

The length of the rod is about 60 diameters of the rocket, and the composition with which the cylinder is filled consists generally of saltpetre, sulphur, and charcoal or gunpowder. The composition is rammed into the case, but a void space is left about the axis, in order that a considerable surface may be at once in a state of combustion. At the choke or neck of the rocket there are several apertures, at one of which the fire is communicated to the composition.

The cause of the rocket's motion is, the excess of the pressure produced by the burning material at the head of the rocket above the pressure at the neck, when *part of the flame* escapes through the apertures; the stick serves to guide the rocket in its flight.

Shells are hollow shot with a hole to receive the fuse; they are discharged, usually, from mortars and howitzers, and are charged with a quantity of powder sufficient to burst them when at the end of their range; the fuze being cut of such a length that the charge may be ignited at the proper moment.

To breach earthen works, the shells are fired horizontally, from howitzers, with reduced charges, that the fuze may not be extinguished before igniting the powder in the shell: this powder is a bursting charge.

Carcasses are shells with three fuze holes; they are filled with a a peculiar composition, which flames out of the holes with great power and fury for about ten minutes: they are thrown from mortars, howitzers, and guns, to set fire to buildings, and sometimes to serve as light balls.

Shrapnell shells, or spherical-case shot, are shells filled with musket balls, having a bursting charge of powder mixed with them.

---

* The former are for signals, and the latter are for military service.

They are discharged from guns and howitzers, and have a fuze like that of a common shell, but shorter, in order that the shell may burst in the air before the completion of its range; in this manner musket balls and the splinters of the shell can be poured into a column of troops at 1,200 yards distance.

Common case, or canister shot, are cylindrical tin canisters with wooden or iron bottoms, containing from 12 to 70 shot, which vary in weight from 1½ oz. to 8 oz. each, according to the calibre of the gun. As they burst nearly at the mouth of the gun, their effect cannot be depended on beyond 200 yards, although they are used at a greater distance.

Grape shot are of two patterns; either the balls are quilted round an iron pin with a circular plate at the bottom, or a pin runs through a succession of plates, between every two of which is a tier of balls; in the latter case they are also called "tier shot."

In the first pattern, the shot soon corrode the canvas quilting, therefore the second is preferred: there are 9 shot in each round, each shot varying in weight from 8 oz. to 4 ℔s. according to the calibre of the gun; the most effective range is about 200 yards.

Hand grenades are shells of about 1 ℔. 13 oz. weight, with a fuze and bursting charge; they can be thrown by the hand, about 25 or 30 yards; they are useful for the defence of breaches and unflanked works.

Gunpowder is composed of 75 parts saltpetre, 15 charcoal, and 10 sulphur in every hundred parts: a cubic foot of it weighs about 55 ℔s.

A shell fuze is a funnel-shaped tube of well-seasoned beech, filled with a composition of saltpetre, sulphur, and mealed gunpowder.

Portfire is a composition of saltpetre, charcoal, and sulphur, pressed closely into a cylinder of white brown paper: they are made in lengths of 16 inches, and are used to discharge guns, to ignite bags of powder, &c.

Portfire and shell fuzes burn at the rate of one inch in five seconds: Bickford's fuze (which will burn under water) burns 6 inches in 5 seconds, or 2 yards in a minute.

To fire shot or shells á ricochet, or in such a manner that they make several bounds during their course, it is necessary to give the gun or howitzer a charge, and an elevation depending on the extent of the range required. In enfilading a work ricochet, the gun should be placed nearly in the direction of the interior slope of the parapet produced; and its elevation should be such that the shot may just clear the crest of the parapet in front.

Ricochet firing against guns in a work, is useless if carried on at a greater distance than 650 yards; the best range is about 400 yards.

Round shot are sometimes fired red hot from heavy guns, to set on fire buildings, blockhouses, shipping, and any defences in the construction of which timber has been employed.

It requires about three-quarters of an hour to heat a 24 pound shot when the furnace has been previously prepared; double that time if not. In loading, a tight dry wad is placed over the powder, and afterwards a wet wad, first soaked, and then well wrung; next, the gun being slightly elevated, the shot is brought up, by means of an instrument called the carrier, and rolled home; if it is required to depress the gun, another wet wad must be placed over the shot.

A gun platform is a flooring of wood or stone, to prevent the wheels or trucks of a gun carriage from sinking into the ground: the garrison and siege platforms are 10 feet wide at the head, 15 feet long, and 14 feet wide at the splay or tail.

CHAPTER III.

MANUAL FOR LIGHT ARTILLERY.

1. For instruction in the manual of light artillery, the piece selected is the light 12-pdr. howitzer, used for mountain service, on account of its simplicity, and as embracing all the principles required for serving a light field piece. It is generally transported by mules. The piece and the shafts may be packed upon one mule, the carriage upon another, and the ammunition chest upon the third. The carriage is adapted for draught.

In case the pieces are served by a fully organized company, a jumper or short light pole, with a cross-piece of iron at the end, is substituted for the shafts. A rope, attached to the axle-tree and running through rings in the cross-piece, enables the detachments to draw the pieces. In coming into battery, the rope is detached and held in a coil ready for use.

2. The mule that draws the piece, or carries it when packed, is called the *shaft mule;* the mule that carries the carriage, when packed, the *carriage mule;* and the mule on which the ammunition chests are packed, the *ammunition mule.*

3. *The piece is in battery* when the shafts are detached and it is in a proper position to be fired. The front in this case is the direction towards which the muzzle points. The front, when the shafts are attached, is the direction towards which the shaft point. The right of the piece, in both cases, is the right of the cannoneer when facing to the front.

The position of the mules, when the piece is in battery, is as follows:

The ammunition mule fifteen yards in rear of the piece, the shaft mule two yards in rear of the ammunition mule, and the carriage mule two yards in rear of the shaft mule, all facing towards the piece.

4. *In the order of march, with the howitzer mounted on its carriage,* the shaft mule is hitched in, and the carriage and ammunition mules follow; the first two yards from the piece, and the second two yards from the first.

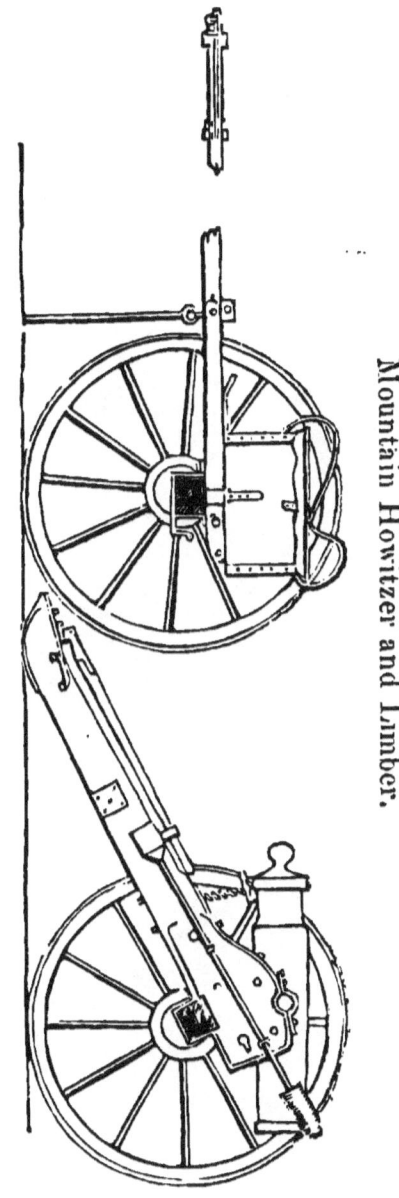

Mountain Howitzer and Limber.

Page 50.

5. *In the order of march, with the piece and carriage packed upon the mules,* the shaft mule leads, and the other two follow; the distance between each being two yards.

FORMING THE DETACHMENT.

6. Six men are required for the service of the piece. They are formed in two ranks, and told off from the right by the chief of piece; Nos. 1 and 2 being on the right, No. 3 and the gunner being in the centre, and Nos. 4 and 5 on their left; the even numbers and the gunner being in the front, and the odd numbers in the rear rank.

The detachment is marched to the piece, and posted as follows:

POSTS OF THE DETACHMENTS.

7. *In battery.* Nos. 1 and 2 about one yard outside of the wheels, and in line with the axle-tree, No. 1 being on the right, and No. 2 on the left; the gunner at the end of the trail; No. 3 opposite the knob of the cascable, covering No. 1; No. 4 on the right, and No. 5 on the left of the ammunition mule; all facing to the front. The chief of piece is opposite to the trail, outside of and near the left cannoneers.

8. *In battery, without mules.* Nos. 4 and 5 are on the right and left of the ammunition chests, facing to the front.

9. *In the order of march, shaft mules hitched in.* Nos. 1 and 2 opposite to the muzzle; the gunner and No. 3 opposite to the trail; and Nos. 4 and 5 opposite to the saddle of the ammunition mule; the gunner and even numbers on the right, and the odd numbers on the left; all facing to the front, and covering each other in lines one yard from the wheels. The chief of piece is on the left of the driver of the shaft mule.

10. *In the order of march, mules packed.* Nos. 1 and 2 at the shaft mule; the gunner and No. 3 at the carriage mule; and Nos. 4 and 5 at the ammunition mule; the gunner and even numbers on the right and odd numbers on the left; all opposite to the saddles, one yard from the mules, and facing to the front. The chief of piece is on the left of the driver of the shaft mule.

11. There is one driver to each mule. He is on the left of the mule, and holds the reins with the right hand, six inches from the mouth, the hand high and firm.

SERVICE OF THE PIECE.

12. The piece is in battery, the men at their posts. (No. 7.)

The shafts are placed on the ground, one yard and a half from the line of the right wheel, and parallel to it, the cross-bar opposite to the trail, the shafts pointing to the rear.

The chests, when the ammunition mule is absent, are on the ground, fifteen yards in rear of the trail, their sides parallel to the axis of the piece, backs together, the turnbuckles outside.

13. At the command TAKE EQUIPMENTS, the gunner distributes the equipments. No. 1, with the assistance of No. 3, takes out the sponge. The gunner equips himself with the belt containing the hausse and priming wire, and with the knee-guard and the finger-stall, wearing the last on the second finger of the left hand. No. 3 wears the tube pouch containing friction tubes and the lanyard. Nos. 1 and 2 wear bricoles hung from the left shoulder to the right side. Nos. 2 and 5 wear haversacks hung from the right shoulder to the left side.

THE COMMANDS.

14. In loading by detail, the instructor gives all the commands. The commands are: *Load by detail*, LOAD, 2, 3, 4; SPONGE, 2, 3, 4; RAM, 2, 3; READY; FIRE; and CEASE FIRING.

When the service of the piece is not executed by detail, the commands of the instructor are, either LOAD, COMMENCE FIRING, and CEASE FIRING; or, COMMENCE FIRING and CEASE FIRING. After the command COMENCE FIRING, the action is continued without further commands from the instructor until the command CEASE FIRING.

The last command is repeated by the chief of piece and the gunner.

DUTIES OF THE CANNONEERS.

15. *Duties of the Gunner.*—In action, the gunner gives or repeats the commands of execution. At the command or signal to commence firing, he gives the word LOAD; plants the left foot opposite to the knob of the cascable; places the right knee upon the ground near, and on the left of the trail; places the hausse, when it is used; seizes the lunette with the right hand, to give the direc-

tion, and at the same time tends vent with the second finger of the left hand, the thumb on the base of the breech.

As soon as the piece is loaded and aimed, he removes the hausse; then rising pricks the cartridge; gives the word READY, and stepping clear of the wheel to the side whence he can best observe the effect of the shot, gives the command, FIRE. He continues the action in the same manner, without farther commands from the instructor, until the firing is ordered to cease.

When the instructor, instead of giving the command COMMENCE FIRING, gives that of LOAD, the gunner repeats it, and performs the same duties as just described, except that he does not command FIRE, until the firing is ordered to commence.

When the instructor gives all the commands, the gunner performs the same duties, but without repeating the commands.

16. *Duties of No. 1.*—Until the command LOAD, he stands square to the front, in line with the axle-tree, holding the sponge staff about the middle in the right hand, and trailing it at an angle of 45°.

For the convenience of instruction, the duties of No. 1 are divided into motions.

First motion.—At the command LOAD, No. 1 faces to his left, steps obliquely to his right with the right foot, and brings the sponge into a perpendicular position over the right toe, the elbow close to the side, the right hand at the height of the elbow.

Second motion.—He plants the left foot near, and in line with the wheel, and inclines the sponge across the body to the left, the right opposite to the middle of the body.

Third motion.—He places the right foot twelve inches to the right of the left, heels on the same line; brings the sponge into a horizontal position, and extending the hands towards the ends of the staff, back of the right hand up, that of the left down, rests the sponge-head against the face of the piece; the knees straight, the feet turned out equally, and the body inclined forward.

Fourth motion.—He introduces the sponge, drops the left hand by the side of his thigh, and shoves the sponge to the bottom of the chamber.

17. At the command SPONGE, he carefully sponges out the chamber.

Second motion.—He draws out the sponge, pressing it upon the bottom of the bore, seizes the staff near the sponge-head with the left hand, back down, and rests it against the face of the piece.

Third motion.—He turns the sponge over by bringing the hands together at the middle of the staff, and giving it a cant with each, throws the sponge over; at the same time turning the wrists so as to bring the staff horizontal. He then extends the hands towards the ends of the staff, back of the left up, that of the right down.

Fourth motion.—As soon as the charge is inserted he introduces the rammer-head into the muzzle, and joins the left hand to the right.

18. At the command RAM, he sends the charge carefully home, throwing the left hand over the piece.

Second motion.—He draws out the sponge with the right hand, letting it slide through the hand as far as the middle of the staff, when he grasps it firmly, and seizing it close to the rammer-head with the left hand, back up, rests it against the face of the piece.

Third motion.—He raises the sponge to the height of his breast, and steps back, right foot first, to his position opposite to the axle-tree; quits the staff with the left hand, and throwing the sponge uppermost, holds it at a trail in the right. He remains facing the piece until the command LOAD, when he steps up and performs the duties just described.

When the loading is not by detail, No. 1 goes through all his duties at the command LOAD.

At the flash of the gun, or command LOAD, he steps up and again performs his duties as before, and so on, until the command CEASE FIRING is given. At this command he resumes his post, faces to the front, first sponging out the piece if it has been commenced.

19. *Duties of Nos. 2 and 5.*—Until the command LOAD, Nos. 2 and 5 stand square to the front, the former in line with the axle-tree, the latter on the left of the ammunition mule, or chests.

At this command, No. 2 faces about and goes to the ammunition chest; and No. 5, having received a round of ammunition from No. 4, carries it to the piece; placing himself opposite to No. 1, and in line with the wheel, inserts the charge as soon as No. 1 has sponged, then steps back to the post of No. 2, opposite to the axle-tree, and there remains facing the piece until it is fired, when he returns to the ammunition chest, No. 2; having received a round of ammunition, carries it to within five yards of the wheel, where he remains until the piece is fired; he then moves forward and executes the remainder of the service as just described for No. 5.

Nos. 2 and 5, in moving to and from the piece, go at a run and pass each other by the right.

In inserting the charge they should be careful to keep the seam down, and to place the fuze in the axis of the bore.

At the command CEASE FIRING, they resume their posts, facing to the front.

20. *Duties of No. 3.*—No. 3 holds the handle of the lanyard in the right hand, the cord passing between the fingers, the hook between the forefinger and thumb. At the command LOAD, he takes a friction tube in the left hand, and passes the hook of the lanyard through the eye of the tube from right to left, continuing to hold the hook between the thumb and forefinger. At the word READY, he faces the piece, and steps up, keeping outside of the wheel; inserts the tube, steps back with the right foot, breaks to his rear a full pace with the left foot, and holds the lanyard slightly stretched, the handle at the height of the knee, back of the hand up, the left hand against the thigh. At the command FIRE, he gives a smart pull upon the lanyard, being careful to keep the hand low, and then resumes his post.

At the command CEASE FIRING, he winds the lanyard upon its handle, and if dry, puts it in the tube pouch.

21. *Duties of No. 4.*—No. 4 attends at the ammunition chest, serves out ammunition, and prepares and inserts fuses.

CHANGING POSTS.

22. In order to instruct the men in all the duties at the piece, the instructor causes them to change posts by the following commands:

1. *Change Posts.* 2. MARCH.

At the first command, the cannoneers on the right of the piece face about, take off their equipments, and place them on the piece or ammunition chests. At the second command, all step off, each taking the post and equipments of the one in his front; No. 2 passing around the muzzle to gain the post of No. 1, and No. 4 around the ammunition chest to take that of No. 5.

23. During the intervals of rest, the instructor will explain to the men the nomenclatures of the piece and carriage, and the names and uses of the implements and equipments.

SERVICE OF THE PIECE WITH DETACHMENTS OF DIFFERENT STRENGTHS.

24. *Two men.* The gunner commands, tends vent, points, pricks, primes, and fires. No. 1 sponges, serves ammunition, and loads.

Three men. The gunner commands, tends vent, points, pricks, primes, and fires. No. 1 sponges. No. 2 serves ammunition, and loads.

Four men. The gunner commands, tends vent, points and pricks. No. 1 sponges. No. 2 serves ammunition, and loads. No. 3 primes and fires.

Five Men. No. 4 attends at the chests, and serves ammunition to No. 2, occasionally alternating with him. The other numbers serve as with four men.

Six men. No. 5 alternate habitually with No. 2. No. 4 remains at the chests. The other numbers serve as with four men.

THE LOCKING ROPE.

25. The locking rope is habitually coiled and suspended from the front arc of the saddle of the shaft mule. When it becomes necessary to use it in order to prevent the too great recoil of the piece, No. 2, on receiving orders to that effect, brings it up from the mule, and, with the assistance of No. 1, locks the wheels. No. 2 attaches one end of it by a timber hitch to the felly of the left wheel, near the ground, and No. 1 attaches the other end in the same manner to the right wheel, the rope passing over the stock.

The length of the rope should be regulated by the nature of the ground.

When in firing it becomes necessary to run the piece forward, the locking rope is detached; No. 2 carries it; and it is re-attached as soon as the piece is in battery. When not in use it is placed on the ground, outside of and near No. 2.

When the firing is to be discontinued, No. 2 returns it to its place on the saddle. The locking rope should not be used when it can be avoided; since on rough ground it is liable to break the wheels, and on soft ground to upset the carriage.

ATTACHING AND DETACHING THE SHAFTS.

26. To attach the shafts, the instructor commands:

ATTACH SHAFTS.

The gunner raises the trail; No. 3 springs in between the shafts, seizes them about twelve inches from the cross-bar, and places the supporting bar upon the trail; the gunner then puts in the key and lowers the trail to the ground. No. 1, with the assistance of No. 3, puts up the sponge; and the cannoneers about the piece assume their posts as in the order of march, shaft mule hitched in.

27. To detach the shafts, the instructor commands:

DETACH SHAFTS.

The gunner raises the trail, and unkeys the shafts; No. 3 springs in between them, seizes them about twelve inches from the crossbar, (the gunner at the same time lowering the trail to the ground,) detaches, and places them as prescribed in No. 12.

No. 1, with the assistance of No. 3, takes out the sponge; and the cannoneers about the piece take their posts as in battery.

MOVING THE PIECE BY MEANS OF THE CANNONEERS.

28. *The shafts detached.* The instructor commands:

    1. *By hand to the front (or rear.)* 2. MARCH.

At the first command Nos. 1 and 2, facing to the front, (or rear,) apply themselves to the wheels with the hand nearest to the piece, the former carrying the sponge, and the latter the locking rope in the hand farthest from the piece; the gunner raises the trail.

At the second command, all step off. At the command, HALT, they resume their posts.

29. *When bricoles are to be used, the shafts attached.* The instructor commands:

    1. *By bricoles to the front (or rear.)* 2. MARCH.

At the first command, Nos. 1 and 2 attach the hooks of their bricoles to the washerhooks, and hold the rope with the hand nearest to the piece; the gunner and No. 3 apply themselves to the shafts; all facing in the direction they are to move.

At the second command, all step off.

At the command, HALT, they resume their posts; Nos. 1 and 2 unhooking their bricoles with the hand nearest to the piece.

30. *Without bricoles, the shafts attached.* The instructor commands:

    1. *Forward.* 2. MARCH.

At the first command, the gunner and No. 3 apply themselves to the shafts; Nos. 1 and 2 at the wheels, as in No. 28.

At the second command, all step off. At the command, HALT, they resume their posts.

When the movement requires it, Nos. 4 and 5 carry the ammunition chests to their new position.

No. 3 carries the shafts when they are detached.

SERVICE OF SEVERAL PIECES.

31. Forming, and marching the detachments to and from the pieces, are executed as in field artillery.

POSTING AND CHANGING THE POSITION OF DETACHMENTS.

32. *To form the order of march, the detachments being in line in front.* The instructor commands:

1. *Detachments, to your posts.* 2. MARCH.

At the first command, the chiefs of pieces face the detachments to the right. At the second, the detachments, Nos. 1 and 2 opening out, file to their posts, each member halting at his place. The chiefs of pieces face them to the front by the command, ABOUT FACE.

To form the order of march, the detachments being in line, in rear, the instructor gives the same commands.

At the first command, the chiefs of pieces face the detachments to the left, at the second, the detachments march to their posts; each number halting as before.

33. *From the order of march, to the front (or rear.)* The instructor commands:

1. *Detachments front (or rear.)* 2. MARCH.

To the front. At the second command, repeated by the chiefs of pieces, the detachments, No. 3 and the gunner closing to the centre when clear of the mule, march to the front, file to the left, and are halted, and faced to the front by the chiefs of pieces.

To the rear. At the first command, the chiefs of pieces face the detachments about, Nos. 4 and 5 standing fast. At the second command, the detachments, Nos. 1 and 2 closing to the centre as they advance, march to the rear, file to the left, are halted and faced to the front by the chiefs of pieces. In both cases Nos. 4 and

5 take their places on the left, when the detachment is in the position ordered.

HITCHING AND UNHITCHING.

34. *To the front.* The instructor commands:

Hitch to the front.

At this command, the shafts are attached, (No. 26,) and the gunner and No. 3 bring the piece about, each by means of the shaft on his own side.

The mule, passing on the right of the piece, is led by its driver to the front and hitched in, the driver backing the mule and buckling the breast straps to the staples; the gunner and No. 3 buckling the thill straps around the shafts through the staples, and the breech straps to the staples.

35. *To the right (or left.)* The instructor commands:

Hitch to the right (or left.)

At this command the shafts are attached, and turned in the proper direction, and the mule, inclining to the right or left, is led to its place, and hitched in as before.

36. *To the rear.* The instructor commands:

Hitch to the rear.

At this command, the shafts are attached, the mule brought up, faced about, and hitched in as before.

37. In hitching in to the front, the carriage and ammunition mules, the former first passing the latter, are led up to their proper positions.

In hitching in to the right, (or left,) the mules are, in like manner, led up and wheeled to the right or left, at the proper intervals.

In hitching in to the rear, the carriage and ammunition mules, following the shaft mule in the order named, are led past the piece to their position in the rear.

For the position of the mules, see No. 3.

UNHITCHING AND COMING INTO ACTION.

38. *To the front.* The instructor commands:

Action Front.

At this command, the mule is unhitched, the driver unbuckling the breast straps, and the gunner and No. 3 the breech and thill straps. The driver then leads the mule to its place in rear, and the gunner and No. 3, supporting the shafts till the mule is taken out, bring the piece about. This done, the shafts are detached and placed as above.

The carriage and ammunition mules are led at once to their positions, (see No. 3.)

39. *To the right, left, or rear.* The instructor commands:

Action right, (left, or rear.)

At this command, the mule is unhitched; the piece placed in the required direction; the shafts detached, and each mule led to its proper position.

In action rear, the carriage and ammunition mules pass by the right of the piece to their places in rear. The mules face towards the piece as in action front.

PACKING AND UNPACKING.

40. *The mule unhitched, and shafts detached.* The instructor commands:

1. *Prepare to pack the Piece.* 2. PACK THE PIECE.

At the first command, the driver leads the shaft mule three yards in rear of the piece, the crupper towards the trail; No. 1, after removing the right cap square, takes the sponge and inserts the rammer head to the bottom of the bore; and No. 2, after removing the left cap square, takes the handspike, and passing one end to No. 3, places it under the knob of the cascable, the loop around the neck. All face towards the mule and prepare to raise the piece.

At the second command, they raise the piece, No. 1 inclining slightly to his left to clear the wheel, and place it upon the saddle, the trunnions in their beds, the vent up, and the cascable towards the head of the mule. No. 1, then withdrawing the sponge, places it, and the handspike which he receives from No. 2, upon the carriage, and goes to the shafts. No. 3, with the assistance of No. 2, secures the piece firmly to the saddle by means of the lashing rope.

For this purpose he passes one end of the rope (the other being fastened to the near hook of the lashing girt) over the piece to No. 2, who passes it back beneath the transoms, receives it again over the piece, and then fastens it, drawing the rope tightly to the off hook of the lashing girth. This done, No. 1 turns the shafts round and carries them near the mule, and Nos. 2 and 3 seizing them near the cross-bar, with the assistance of No. 1 acting at the ends, raise and place them upon the mule, resting the cross-bar upon the cascable, and the shafts upon the arcs; Nos. 2 and 3, the latter first putting the key in its place, then secure the shafts firmly by means of the lashing straps.

PACKING THE CARRIAGE UPON THE MULE.

41. The instructor commands:

1. *Prepare to pack the Carriage.* 2. PACK THE CARRIAGE.

At the first command, the driver leads the carriage mule in front of the carriage, and three yards from it, the crupper towards the head of the carriage; the gunner, first replacing the cap squares, raises the head of the carriage, and Nos. 4 and 5, at the right and left wheels respectively, remove the linchpins and washers, take off the wheels, and lay them on the ground behind them, the larger end of the nave uppermost. This done, Nos. 4 and 5 replace the linchpins and washers, and seize the arms of the axle-tree; and the gunner, quitting the head of the carriage, seizes the trail; all face towards the mule, and prepare to raise the carriage.

At the second command, they raise the carriage and place it upon the saddle, between the transoms; the axle-tree just in front of the forward arc, the understraps upon the arc, and the nuts of the trunnion plate bolts just in rear of it. The carriage having been placed, No. 4, with the assistance of No. 5, secures it with the lashing cord, taking two turns with the cord round the stock and transoms, and then tying it. This done, they suspend the wheels by the fellies, from the arms of the axle trees; the large end of the nave between the arcs, and resting against the leather of the outside bar, and secure them firmly by means of the lashing straps.

The whole is then strongly bound by the lashing rope. For this purpose, No. 5, having fastened one end to the near hook of the lashing girth, passes the rope up from the inside between the nearest convenient felly and spoke, and continues it on, pressing it in front of and against the outside part of the nave, embracing one or more spokes, to the top felly, under which, and over the stock, he passes it to No. 4, who, after passing it round a spoke of the off wheel, returns it under the transoms of the saddle to No. 5 by whom it is passed round a spoke and again handed over the stock to No. 4. The latter then carries it down under the top felly, around the spokes, and against the nave, as with the near wheel, to the off hook of the lashing girth, and then fastens it.

For greater security, the gunner may tie the fellies of the two wheels together, behind the elevating screw, with the locking rope.

PACKING THE AMMUNITION CHESTS UPON THE MULE.

42. The instructor commands:

1. *Prepare to pack the Chests.* 2. PACK THE CHESTS.

At the first command, the driver leads the mule from the rear to the distance of one yard from the chests, its head still facing them; Nos. 2 and 4 hasten to the chest on the right, and Nos. 1 and 5 to that on the left, and seize them by the handles; Nos. 1 and 2 by those in front, and Nos. 4 and 5 by those in rear.

At the second command, they raise the chests, carry them to the saddle, and attach the chains to the hooks, the chests inclining slightly towards the rear of the mule; Nos. 4 and 5 then secure them with the lashing straps and lashing rope.

This duty might be done with three men, by first hooking on one chest, and letting one man support it until the other is hooked on.

PACKING THE MULES AT ONE COMMAND.

43. The instructor commands:

Pack the mules.

At this command, the driver leads the mules to their proper positions; Nos. 1, 2, and 3 proceed to pack the piece, and Nos. 4, 5, and the gunner the carriage, as soon as the piece is removed. This done, Nos. 1, 2, 4, and 5 pack the ammunition chests.

Each cannoneer performs his duty as directed in Nos. 40, 41, 42.

UNPACKING THE CARRIAGE.

44. The instructor commands:

1. *Prepare to unpack the Carriage.* 2. UNPACK THE CARRIAGE.

At the first command, Nos. 4 and 5 unbuckle the lashing straps, detach the lashing rope, take off the wheels, and lay them upon the ground, the large end of the nave uppermost. If the locking rope has been used, the gunner unties and detaches it. Nos. 4 and 5 then untie and remove the lashing cord, and facing to the rear, seize the arms of the axle-tree; the gunner facing to the front seizes the trail. All prepare to raise the carriage.

At the second command, they raise the carriage, and carry it three yards in rear of the mule; the gunner then, placing the trail upon the ground, seizes the head of the carriage and holds it up; Nos. 4 and 5, removing the linchpins and washers, retain them in their hands, put on the wheels, and then replace the linchpins and washers. The gunner puts up the locking rope, and Nos. 4 and 5 the lashing rope.

UNPACKING THE PIECE.

45. The instructor commands:

1. *Prepare to unpack the Piece.* 2. UNPACK THE PIECE.

At the first command, the driver leads the mule in rear of and three yards from the carriage, the crupper towards the trail; Nos. 2 and 3 unbuckle the lashing straps, and, with the assistance of No. 1 acting at the ends, disengage the shafts from the saddle; No. 1 then takes hold of them near the cross-bar, turns them round, and lays them on the ground, in the position described in No. 12. This done, Nos. 2 and 3 detach the lashing rope; and No. 1, having taken the sponge and handspike, hands the latter to No. 2, and inserts the former into the bore of the piece. No. 2 then applies his handspike as in No. 40; when all, facing towards the carriage, prepare to raise the piece.

At the second command, they raise the piece, No. 1 inclining slightly to his right to clear the wheel, and place it upon its carriage. No. 1 puts up the sponge, No. 2 the handspike, and No. 3 secures the cap squares.

UNPACKING THE AMMUNITION CHESTS.

46. The instructor commands:

1. *Prepare to unpack the Chests.* 2. UNPACK THE CHESTS.

At the first command, Nos. 2 and 4 seize the handles of the right chest, and Nos. 1 and 5 those of the left: Nos. 4 and 5 having first unbuckled the lashing straps, and detached the lashing rope.

At the second command, they raise the chests, unhook them, and lay them on the ground one yard from the mule.

UNPACKING THE MULES AT ONE COMMAND.

47. The instructor commands:

Unpack the mules.

At this command, the drivers place the shaft and carriage mules eight yards apart, the crupper towards the place the piece is to occupy; the gunner, and Nos. 4 and 5 proceed to unpack the carriage, and Nos. 1, 2, and 3 the piece. The sponge and handspike are not taken from the carriage until it is on the ground, nor is the piece taken from the saddle until the carriage is mounted on its wheels. Each cannoneer performs his duty as directed in Nos. 44 and 45.

If the ammunition chests are to be unpacked, it is done as soon as the piece is mounted, as prescribed in No. 46.

CHAPTER IV.

MANUAL FOR HEAVY ARTILLERY.

SERVICE OF THE PIECE.

1. The manner of serving heavy artillery varies with the kind of piece, and the carriage upon which it is mounted.

2. There are four kinds of heavy pieces in the land service, viz.: the GUN, the HOWITZER, the MORTAR, and the COLUMBIAD.

They are distinguished according to their use, as *siege, garrison,* and *sea-coast artillery.*

For their service six distinct kinds of carriages are necessary, viz: the *siege,* the *barbette,* the *casemate,* the *flank-casemate,* the *columbiad,* and the carriage upon which the MORTAR is mounted, which is technically called its *bed.*

Siege artillery is used in the attack of places; and as it follows armies in their operations, is mounted upon carriages which serve for its transportation.

Garrison artillery is employed in the defence of forts, more especially those of the interior; and *sea-coast artillery,* consisting of the heaviest calibres, is used for the defence of the sea-coast. Their carriages do not subserve the purpose of transportation; the barbette carriage may, however, be used for moving its piece for short distances, as from one front of a work to another.

The following are the kinds and calibres of HEAVY ARTILLERY used in the land service of the United States:

Kind of Ordnance.		Calibre.	Material.
Guns.	Siege and Garrison.	12-pdr. 18-pdr. 24-pdr.	Iron.
	Sea-coast.	32-pdr. 42-pdr.	
Howitzers.	Siege and Garrison.	8-inch. 24-pdr.	
Columbiads.	Sea-coast.	8-inch. 10-inch.	
Mortars.		8-inch. 10-inch.	
	Siege.	8-inch. 10-inch.	
	Sea-coast.	10-inch. 13-inch.	
	Stone.	16-inch.	Bronze.
	Cohorn.	24-pdr.	

3. The detachment for serving a piece is formed in two ranks, and numbered from right to left. The odd numbers from the rear rank, and serve on the right of the piece; the even numbers and the gunner form the front rank, and serve on its left. The right file is numbered 1 and 2; the next file 3 and 4; the gunner is uncovered, and generally on the left of No. 4; and on his left are as many files as are deemed necessary, numbered 5 and 6, 7 and 8, etc.

4. A piece is in battery when it is in the proper position to be fired.

The right of a piece, when in battery, is the right of the cannoneer when facing to the object to be fired at; the front is the direction towards which the muzzle points.

The term *battery* is applied to one or more pieces, or to the places where the pieces are fired.

A *platform* is the support upon which a piece is manœuvred when in battery.

5. The detachment is marched to the battery by a flank. It is halted, and faced to the front, when its centre is opposite to the middle of the platform, and (if there be room) four yards from it.

6. To cause the cannoneers to take their posts, the instructor commands:

1. *Detachment, to your posts.* 2. MARCH.

At the first command, the detachment is faced to the right by the chief of piece.

At the second command, it files to the left, and the two flanks separate; the rear rank marching to the right of the piece, and the front rank to the left, in lines parallel to its axis. As each man arrives at his post, he halts and faces to the piece; Nos. 1 and 2 one yard from the epaulment, parapet, or scarp, their breasts eighteen inches outside of the wheels of the carriage or cheeks of the mortar bed, as the case may be; and the other numbers and the gunner, dressing on Nos. 1 and 2 respectively at intervals of one yard, except that between Nos. 3 and 5 there is an interval of two yards. With the mortar, Nos. 1 and 2 are opposite to the front manœuvring bolts, and Nos. 3 and 4 opposite to those in the rear.

Under the fire of the enemy, the men will be directed to cover themselves by the parapet as much as may be consistent with the execution of their duties.

7. *The chief of piece* (a non-commissioned officer) assists the instructor in effecting a correct execution of the movements. While at the battery, he will generally be one yard outside of the cannoneers of the left, facing the piece, and two yards in rear of the platform or rearmost part of the carriage. He communicates and attends to the execution of all orders he may receive in relation to the service of his piece; as, for instance, the kind of ammunition to be used, the weight of charge, the kind and length of fuze, etc.

8. The movements of the cannoneers at the battery are in *double quick time*.

9. Posts are changed at the discretion of the instructor.

10. To allow the detachment to rest, the instructor commands:

In place. REST; or, REST.

The cannoneers lay down their handspikes.

In the first case, the men remain at their posts; in the second case, they may leave their posts, but will remain near the piece.

To resume the exercise, the instructor commands:

Attention—DETACHMENT.

At which command, all resume their posts and handspikes.

11. Until the cannoneer becomes well versed in his duties at the piece, the instructor will himself, by way of example, occasionally execute the movements which he orders. In the intervals of rest he will minutely instruct the men in the names and uses of the implements, and in the nomenclatures of the piece, its carriage or bed, and of the parts of the fortification near the battery. In the course of the instruction, he will require every man to point out and designate by name all the parts enumerated in these nomenclatures, and to answer questions relative to the service of the piece; such as the weight of charge, the manner of making cartridges and wads, of heating shot and throwing hot shot, of laying platforms, pointing, etc. And although he is to consider precision of movement as highly essential, yet he is to inculcate that something more is necessary than a merely mechanical performance of duty. He will, therefore, endeavor to impress upon the cannoneer not only the habit of a soldier-like manner of working his gun, but an accurate understanding of all the elements necessary to the efficiency of its fire.

12. To leave the battery, the instructor commands:

1. *Detachment, rear.* 2. MARCH.

At the first command, the detachment is faced from the epaulment by the chief of piece.

At the second command, it marches to the rear—the cannoneers of the left closing upon those of the right—files to the right, and is halted and faced to the front by the chief of piece, so as to bring its centre opposite to the middle of the platform, and four yards from it. The chief of piece places himself upon the right.

The detachment is marched from the battery by a flank.

LESSON I.

Service of a Gun mounted on a siege carriage.

Seven men are necessary; one gunner and six other cannoneers.

13. The piece is in battery upon its platform.

The implements, etc., are arranged as follows:

HANDSPIKES, . { Three on each side of the carriage leaning against the epaulment, in line with the cannoneers.

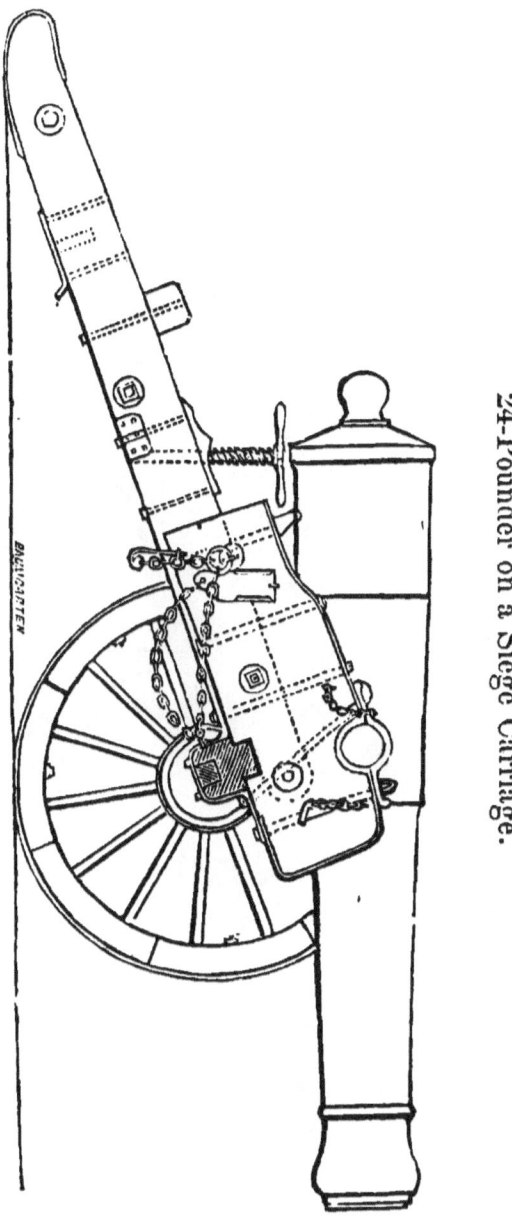

24-Pounder on a Siege Carriage.

Sponge Rammer,	One yard behind and parallel to the line of cannoneers of the right, the sponge uppermost, the sponge and rammer-heads turned from the epaulment, and supported upon a prop.
Pass-box, . .	Against the epaulment, outside of the pile of balls.
Tube-pouch, . .	Containing friction tubes, and the lanyard, which is habitually wound in the form of St. Andrew's cross upon its handle. Suspended from the knob of the cascable.
Gunner's-pouch,	Containing the gunner's level, breech sight, fingerstall, priming wire, gimlet, vent-punch and chalk. Suspended from the knob of the cascable.
Chocks, . . .	One on each side of the piece, near the ends of the hurter.
Vent-cover, . .	Covering the vent.
Tompion, . . .	In the muzzle.
Broom, . . .	Leaning against the epaulment, outside of the pile of balls.

When several guns are served together, there will be only one gunner's level and two vent-punchers to each battery, not exceeding six pieces. To the same battery there will be one *worm*, one *ladle*, and one *wrench*.

The balls are regularly piled on the left of the piece, near the epaulment, and close to the edge of the platform.

The wads are placed between the epaulment and the balls, partly resting on them.

14. The cannoneers having been marched to their posts, the instructor directs them to place their muskets against the epaulment, and then explains to them the names and uses of the implements, and the nomenclatures of the gun, its carriage and the battery.

15. To cause the implements to be distributed, the instructor commands:

Take Implements.

The gunner steps to the knob of the cascable; takes off the vent-cover, handing it to No. 2 to place against the epaulment, outside of the pass-box; gives the tube-pouch to No. 3; equips himself with his own pouch and the fingerstall, wearing the latter on the second finger of the left hand; levels the piece by the elevating screw; applies his level to ascertain the highest points of the base-ring and swell of-the muzzle, which he marks with chalk, and resumes his post.

No. 3 equips himself with the tube-pouch.

Nos. 1 and 2, after passing two handspikes each to Nos. 3 and 4, take each one for himself. Nos. 5 and 6 receives theirs from Nos. 3 and 4.

16. The handspike is held in both hands; the hand nearest to the epaulment grasping it near the small end and at the height of the shoulder, back of the hand down, the arm extended naturally; the butt of the handspike upon the platform on the side farthest from the epaulment, and six inches in advance of the alignment.

17. When the cannoneer lays down his handspike, he places it directly before him, about six inches in advance of and parallel to the alignment, the small end towards the epaulment; and whenever he thus lays it down for the discharge of any particular duty, he will resume it on returning to his post after the completion of that duty.

18. The instructor causes the service of the piece to be executed by the following commands:

1. From Battery.

The gunner moves two paces to his right.

Nos. 1, 2, 3, 4, 5 and 6, facing from the epaulment, unbar; Nos. 1 and 2 under the front of the wheels; Nos. 3 and 4 through the rear spokes of the wheels near the felly, under and perpendicularly to the cheeks; and Nos. 5 and 6 under the manœuvring bolts.

All being ready, the gunner gives the command HEAVE, which will be repeated as often as may be necessary. He sees Nos. 5 and 6 guide the trail in prolongation of the directrix of the embrasure, and as soon as the face of the piece is about one yard from the epaulment, commands HALT. All unbar, and resume their posts, Nos. 1 and 2 chock the wheels.

2. *Load by Detail.* LOAD.

19. Nos. 1, 2 and 4 lay down their handspikes.

No. 2 takes out the tompion, and places it near the vent-cover.

No. 1 faces once and a half to his left; steps over the sponge and rammer; faces to the piece; takes the sponge with both hands, the back down, the right hand three feet from the sponge head, the left hand eighteen inches nearer to it, returns to the piece, entering the staff in the embrasure; places the left foot in line with the face of the piece, half way between it and the wheels; breaks to the right with the right foot, the heels on a line parallel to the direction of the piece, the left leg straightened, the right knee bent, the body erect upon the haunches; and rests the end of the sponge in the muzzle, the staff in the prolongation of the bore, supported by the right hand, the right arm extended, the left hand flat against the side of the thigh.

No. 3 steps to the muzzle, and occupies a position on the left of the piece corresponding to that of No. 1 on its right. He seizes the staff with the left hand, back down, near to and outside of the hand of No. 1.

No. 2, facing towards the epaulment, embars under the breech, and maintains the piece in a convenient position for inserting the sponge, until he receives a signal from the gunner to unbar. He then lays down his handspike; steps over the rammer, and seizes the staff with both hands, as prescribed for the sponge; and stands ready to exchange with No. 1.

No. 4 takes the pass-box and goes to the rear for a cartridge; returns with it, and places himself, facing the piece, about eighteen inches to the rear and right of No. 2.

The gunner places himself near the stock, the left foot advanced, closes the vent with the second finger of the left hand, bending well forward to cover himself by the breech; turns the elevating screw with the right hand, so as to adjust the piece conveniently for loading: and makes a signal for No. 3 to unbar.

20. In the mean time Nos. 1 and 2 insert the sponge by the following motions:

First motion.—They insert the sponge as far as the hand of No. 1, bodies erect, shoulders square.

Second motion.—They slide the hand along the staff, and seize it at arm's length.

Third motion.—They force the sponge down as prescribed in the first motion.

Fourth motion.—They repeat the second motion.

Fifth motion.—They push the sponge to the bottom of the bore. No. 1. replaces the left hand on the staff, back up, six inches nearer to the muzzle than the right. No. 2 places the right hand, back up, between the hands of No. 1.

If in executing these motions, or the corresponding ones with the rammer, it be found that the sponge or rammer is at home at the third or fourth motion, then what is prescribed for the fifth motion will be performed at the third or fourth. The knee on the side towards which the body is to be inclined is always bent, the other straightened; and the weight of the body added, as much as possible, to the effort exerted by the arms.

3. SPONGE.

21. Nos. 1 and 2, pressing the sponge firmly against the bottom of the bore, turn it three times from right to left, and three times from left to right; replace the hands on the thighs; and withdraw the sponge by motions contrary to those prescribed for inserting it.

Remark.—To handle the sponge when it is new and fits tight, it may become necessary for Nos. 1 and 2 to use both hands. In this case it will be inserted and withdrawn by short and quick motions.

No. 2 quits the staff, and turning towards No. 4, receives from him the cartridge, which he takes in both hands, back down, and introduces into the bore bottom foremost, seams to the sides; he then grasps the rammer in the way prescribed for the sponge.

No. 1, rising upon the right leg and turning towards his left, passes the sponge above the rammer with the left hand to No. 3, and receiving the rammer with the right, presents it as prescribed for the sponge, except that he rests the rammer-head against the right side of the face of the piece.

No. 3, as soon as the sponge is withdrawn, passing the rammer under the sponge into the embrasure with the right hand, receives the sponge from No. 1 with the left, replaces it upon the prop, and resumes his post.

No. 4, setting down the pass-box, takes out the cartridge and presents it in both hands to No. 2, the choke to the front, returns the pass-box to its place, and picks up a ball, and afterwards a wad, should one be required.

Nos. 1 and 2 force down the cartridge by the motions prescribed for forcing down the sponge.

4. RAM.

22. Nos. 1 and 2, drawing the rammer out to the full extent of their arms, ram with a single stroke. No. 2 quits the staff, and turning towards No. 4, receives from him the ball and wad, whilst

No. 1 throws out the rammer, and holds the head against the right side of the face of the piece. No. 2, receiving successively the ball and wad, introduces them into the bore, the ball first, and seizes the staff with the left hand. No. 4 then resumes his post.

Nos. 1 and 2 force down the ball and wad together by the same motions, and ram in the same manner as prescribed for the cartridge. No. 2 quits the rammer; sweeps, if necessary, the platform on his own side; passes the broom to No. 1; and resumes his post. No. 1 throws out the rammer, and places it upon the prop below the sponge; finishes the sweeping, and resumes his post.

The gunner pricks, leaving the priming wire in the vent; resumes his post; and, if firing beyond point-blank range, adjusts the breech-sight to the distance.

5. In Battery.

23. Nos. 1 and 2 unchock the wheels, and with Nos. 3, 4, 5, and 6, all facing towards the epaulment, embar ; Nos. 1 and 2 through the front spokes of the wheels near the felly, under and perpendicularly to the cheeks; Nos. 3 and 4 under the rear of the wheels; and Nos. 5 and 6 under the manœuvring bolts perpendicularly to the stock.

All being ready, the gunner commands HEAVE, and the piece is run into battery; Nos. 5 and 6 being careful to guide the chase into the middle of the embrasure.. As soon as the wheels touch the hurter, he commands HALT. All unbar, and Nos. 1, 2, 3, and 4 resume their posts.

6. Point.

24. No. 3 lays down his handspike, passes the hook of the lanyard through the eye of a tube from front to rear, and holds the handle of the lanyard with the right hand, the hook between the thumb and forefinger.

Nos. 5 and 6 embar under and perpendicularly to the trail, near the manœuvring bolts.

The gunner, placing himself at the stock, as at the command LOAD, withdraws the priming-wire, and, aided by Nos. 5 and 6, gives the direction, causing the trail to be moved by commanding LEFT, or RIGHT, tapping at the same time on the right side of the breech for No. 5 to move the trail to the left, or on the left side for No. 6 to move it to the right.

He then places the centre point of the breech-sight accurately upon the chalk mark on the base-ring, and by the elevating screw gives the proper elevation, rectifying the direction, if necessary.

The moment the piece is correctly pointed, he rises on the left leg, and gives the word READY, making a signal with both hands, at which Nos. 5 and 6 unbar, and resume their posts; takes the breech-sight with the left hand, and goes to the windward to observe the effect of the shot.

No. 3 inserts the tube in the vent, drops the handle, allowing the lanyard to uncoil as he steps back to his post, holding it slightly stretched with the right hand, the cord passing between the fingers, back of the hand up; and breaks to the rear a full pace with the left foot, the left hand against the thigh.

At the word READY, Nos. 1 and 2 take the chocks, and breaking off with the feet furthest from the epaulment, stand ready to chock the wheels.

25. In directing the piece to be fired, the instructor will designate it by its number, as, for example:

7. *Number one*—FIRE.

No. 3 gives a smart pull upon the lanyard.

Immediately after the discharge of the piece, Nos. 1 and 2 chock the wheels, and resume the erect position. No. 3 resumes the erect position, and rewinds the lanyard in St. Andrew's cross upon its handle, returning it if dry to the tube-pouch. The gunner, having observed the effect of the shot, returns to his post.

26. Whenever the piece is to be fired by a *lock, port-fire,* or *slow-match,* it will be done by No. 3, as prescribed for No. 4, in the instruction for field artillery.

27. To continue the exercise, the instructor resumes the series of commands, beginning with FROM BATTERY.

TO CHANGE POSTS.

28. To change posts the instructor commands:

1. CHANGE POSTS. 2. MARCH. 3. CALL OFF.

At the first command, the cannoneers lay down their handspikes; place their equipments on the parts of the carriage nearest to them; and face to their left.

MANUAL FOR HEAVY ARTILLERY.   75

At the second command, they step off, each advancing one post; No. 2 taking that of No. 1. Nos. 2 and 5 pass to the rear of the trail; No. 2 on the outside of all the cannoneers. On arriving at their posts, they face to the piece, and equip themselves.

At the third command, they call off, according to the posts they are to occupy.

TO LOAD FOR ACTION.

29. The cannoneers having been sufficiently instructed in the details of the movements, the instructor commands:

Load for action—LOAD.

The piece is run from battery, loaded, run into battery, pointed, and prepared for firing, by the following commands from the gunner: FROM BATTERY—LOAD—IN BATTERY—POINT—READY.

At the command or signal from the instructor to commence firing, the gunner gives the command FIRE, and continues the action until the instructor directs the firing to cease.

TO CEASE FIRING.

30. To cause the firing to cease, the instructor commands:

CEASE FIRING.

Whether the cannoneers are *loading by detail* or *for action*, the piece is sponged out, and all resume their posts. If the cartridge has been inserted, the loading will be completed, unless the instructor should otherwise direct.

TO SECURE PIECE, AND REPLACE IMPLEMENTS.

31. To discontinue the exercise, the instructor having ordered the firing to cease, and caused the piece to be run into battery, gives the following commands:

1. SECURE PIECE.

No. 2 returns the tompion to the muzzle, the gunner puts on the vent-cover, which he receives from No. 2, and depresses the piece.

2. REPLACE IMPLEMENTS.

Nos. 1 and 2 replace the handspikes against the epaulment, those of Nos. 3, 4, 5 and 6 being passed to them by Nos. 3 and 4 for that purpose. The gunner hangs the pouches upon the knob of the cascable.

TO LEAVE THE BATTERY.

32. The instructor causes the muskets to be taken; forms the detachment in rear of the piece; and marches it from the battery as prescribed in No. 12.

33. *Remarks.*—The service of a 24 pdr. siege gun, as it respects running from and to battery, and pointing, is performed by five men, as prescribed for the siege howitzer. Five men suffice for the service of the 18 and 12 pdrs. To perform, however, all the duties incident to a battery of heavy artillery on a war establishment, including transportation and the mechanical manœuvres, the details for its daily service, at three reliefs, should allow at least twenty privates to each piece.

TO SERVE THE PIECE WITH REDUCED NUMBERS.

34. The smallest number of men with which heavy pieces can be served with facility, has been given as five. It may be necessary, however, from the men being disabled, or from other circumstances, to serve a gun with a less number.

With four men.—They will be told off as gunner, and Nos. 1, 2, and 3. In this case No. 2 will, in addition to his own duties, perform those of No. 4.

With three men.—They will be told off as gunner, and Nos. 1 and 2. No. 1 performs the duties prescribed for No. 3, as well as his own. No. 2 performs those of No. 4, as in the preceding case.

When No. 2 serves ammunition, he goes for the cartridge, and places the pass-box behind his post, before assisting No. 1 to sponge.

TRANSPORTATION.

35. The transportation of a 24-pounder gun requires ten horses and five drivers; an 18-pounder eight horses and four drivers; a

battery wagon six horses and three drivers; and spare carriages—at the rate of one for every five pieces require each six horses and three drivers.

CHARGES, ETC.

36. The ordinary service charge of powder for heavy guns is *one-fourth* the weight of the shot. For firing double shot it is *one-sixth* that weight. The breaching charge is *one-third* the weight of the shot.

Range of a 24 pdr., at an angle of 1° 30′, (*point blank*), charge 6 lbs.,	950 yards.
Range of a 24-pdr., at an angle of 5°, charge 6 lbs..	1900 "
Range of an 18-pdr., at an angle of 1° 30′, charge 4½ lbs.,	800 "
Range of an 18-pdr., at an angle of 5°, charge 4½ lbs.,	1600 "
Proof range of powder,	300 "
The range of a 12-pdr. is about the same as that of an 18-pdr.	
Greatest elevation that a 24-pdr. carriage admits,	12°
Greatest elevation that an 18-pdr. carriage admits,	12°
Greatest elevation that a 12-pdr. carriage admits,	13°
Greatest depression that a 24-pdr. carriage admits,	4°
Greatest depression that an 18-pdr. carriage admits,	4°
Greatest depression that a 12-pdr. carriage admits,	4°

WADS.

37. *Wads* are not generally necessary, except when firing at angles of depression; and then only one is used, and that on the ball. When, however, the piece has been fired so often that the ball has caused a *lodgment* in the bore, it is well to use wads differing in length, according to the position and extent of the lodgment, between the shot and the cartridge.

Hay wads may be made by twisting hay into a rope of about one inch in diameter, folding it together of any desired length, and then winding the folds from one end to the other, leaving the wad a little larger than the bore.

BREACHING BATTERIES.

38. *Breaching batteries* established against walls are:

First. To make a horizontal section the length of the desired breach along the scarp, at one-third its height from the bottom of the ditch, and to a depth equal to the thickness of the wall.

Secondly. To make vertical cuts through the wall, not further than ten yards apart, and not exceeding one to each piece; beginning at the horizontal section, and ascending gradually to the top of the wall.

Thirdly. To fire at the most prominent points of the masonry left standing; beginning always at the bottom, and gradually approaching to the top.

Fourthly. To fire into the broken mass with howitzers until the breach is practicable.

Breaches of more than twenty yards in length have been opened by way of experiment, and rendered practicable, in less than ten hours, by about two hundred and thirty 24-pdr. balls and forty shells in one case, and by three hundred 18-pdr. balls and forty shells in another.

RAPIDITY OF FIRING.

39. Iron guns sustain long-continued and rapid firing better than brass guns. A iron gun should sustain twelve hundred discharges, at the rate of twelve an hour; but whatever may be the rate of fire, it is deemed unsafe after that number of discharges. As many as twenty an hour have been made for sixteen consecutive hours.

PENETRATION OF SHOT.

40. The penetration of balls increases to a certain extent with their calibre. The mean result, from several experiments, gives the penetration of a 24-pdr. ball, with the charge of one-third its weight, at the distance of one hundred yards, as follows:

	Feet.	Inches.
In earth of old parapets,	8	6
In earth recently thrown up,	15	0
In oak wood, sound and hard,	4	6
In rubble stone and masonry,	1	10
In brick,	3	0

LESSON II.

Service of an 8-inch Siege Howitzer, mounted on a 24-pdr. Siege Carriage.

Five men are necessary: one gunner and four other cannoneers.

41. The piece is in battery upon its platform.

The implements, ect., are arranged as follows:

HANDSPIKES,	Three on the left of the carriage, and two on the right, leaning against the epaulment, in line with the cannoneers.
SPONGE & RAMMER,	On props, eighteen inches behind and parallel to the cannoneers of the right, the sponge-head turned towards the epaulment.
HAVERSACK,	Containing fuzes, a pair of sleeves, and a priming-wire, bent at right angles at the point for withdrawing the cartridge used in instruction. Suspended from the knob of the cascable.
TUBE-POUCH,	Containing friction tubes, and the lanyard, wound in St. Andrew's cross upon its handle. Suspended from the knob of the cascable.
GUNNERS'-POUCH,	Containing the gunner's level breech-sight, finger-stall, priming-wire, gimlet, vent-punch, and chalk. Suspended from the knob of the cascable.
LOADING-TONGS, QUADRANT, PLUMMET, SCRAPER, WIPER, SPLINTS,	In a basket or on a shelf, against the epaulment, outside of and near the handspikes of the left.
GRUMMET-WAD,	On the end of the hurter, near No. 2.
CHOCKS,	One on each side of the piece, near the ends of the hurter.
VENT-COVER,	Covering the vent.
TOMPION,	In the muzzle.
QUOIN,	Under the breech.
BROOM,	Leaning against the epaulment, outside of the basket or shelf.

When several howitzers are served together, there will be only one gunner's level and two vent-punches to each battery, not exceeding six pieces. To the same battery there will be one wrench.

One shell and one bombazine cartridge bag for instruction—the bag filled with sawdust, and having loops of thread at the choke end—are at the magazine, or other safe place in rear of the piece.

42. The cannoneers having been marched to their posts, the instructor directs them to place their muskets against the epaulment,

and then explains to them the names and uses of the implements, and the nomenclatures of the howitzer, its carriage, and the battery.

43. To cause the implements to be distributed, the instructor commands:

Take Implements.

The gunner steps to the knob of the cascable; takes off the vent-cover, handing it to No. 2 to place against the epaulment, outside of the basket; gives the tube-pouch to No. 3, and the haversack to No. 4; and equips himself with his own pouch and the finger-stall, wearing the latter on the second finger of the left hand.

No. 2 puts on the sleeves.

No. 3 equips himself with the tube-pouch.

No. 4 equips himself with the haversack, which he wears from the right shoulder to the left side; takes out the sleeves; and assists No. 2 to put them on.

Nos. 1 and 2, after passing handspikes to Nos. 3 and 4 and the gunner, take each one for himself. The gunner, receiving his from No. 4, lays it in the allignment, the small end towards the epaulment, and two yards to his right. The other handspikes are held, laid down, and resumed, as prescribed in Nos. 15 and 16.

The gunner directs No. 3 to raise the breech to enable him to level the piece; applies his level to ascertain the highest points of the base-ring and muzzle-band, which he marks with chalk; and resumes his post.

44. The instructor causes the service of the piece to be executed by the following commands:

1. From Battery.

The gunner moves two paces to his right.

Nos. 1, 2, 3, and 4, facing from the epaulment, embar: Nos. 1 and 2 through the rear spokes of the wheels, near the felly, under and perpendicularly to the cheeks; and Nos. 3 and 4 under the manœuvring bolts.

All being ready, the gunner gives the command HEAVE, which will be repeated as often as may be necessary. He sees that Nos. 3 and 4 guide the trail in prolongation of the directrix of the embrasure, and as soon as the wheels are about one yard from the epaulment, commands HALT. All unbar, and resume their posts. Nos. 1 and 2 chock the wheels.

2. *Load by detail*—LOAD.

45. Nos. 1, 2, and 4, lay down their handspikes.

No. 2 takes out the tompion, and places it near the vent-cover; sweeps, if necessary, his side of the platform; passes the broom to the right side of the piece; and resumes his post.

No. 1 faces to his right, and seizes the sponge-staff at its middle with the right hand, back up; places himself at the muzzle; forces the sponge to the bottom of the chamber; and grasps the staff with both hands: all nearly as in field artillery.

No. 3, facing towards the epaulment, embars under the breech or knob of the cascable, until he receives a signal from the gunner to unbar, when he resumes his post.

No. 4 goes to the rear for a cartridge and shell; puts the cartridge in his haversack; takes the shell in both hands; returns and places it on the grummet-wad; and stands, facing the piece, about eighteen inches to the rear and left of No. 2.

The gunner places himself near the stock, as in No. 18, and closes the vent with the second finger of the left hand; adjusts the piece with the quoin to about one degree's elevation; and makes a sign for No. 3 to unbar.

3. SPONGE.

46. No. 1, pressing the sponge firmly against the bottom of the chamber, turns it three times from right to left, and three times from left to right; draws it out to the front of the chamber; wipes out the bore; reinserts the sponge along the upper side of the bore as far as the chamber; draws it entirely out, pressing it upon the lower side of the bore; turns the sponge over towards the embrasure; and presents the rammer-head against the right side of the face of the piece, holding the staff in both hands.

No. 2, as soon as the sponging is completed, takes the tongs and occupies a position at the muzzle corresponding to that prescribed for No. 1 on the right; turns to his left on the right heel, advancing the left foot, and presents the tongs in both hands, the left hand nearest him, the tongs opened, their legs in the same vertical plane.

No. 4 takes out the cartridge and inserts it as far as its middle in the tongs, choke foremost, the seam downwards; removes the stopper from, and inserts the fuze into, the fuze plug; scrapes its end; and takes the wiper.

No. 2, having received the cartridge in the tongs, makes a face and a half to his right on the right heel, and breaks off with the left foot; places the right hand against the head of the left cheek of the carriage, and with the left hand introduces the cartridge into the chamber, keeping the legs of the tongs in a vertical plane; then slightly withdrawing and closing the tongs, he presses them in the direction of the axis of the piece against the end of the cartridge, and shoves it home. Withdrawing the tongs, he makes a face and a half to his left on the right heel, and puts the hooks of the tongs into the ears of the shell, which he lifts and holds about two feet from the ground, whilst No. 4 wipes it.

No. 1, as soon as the tongs are withdrawn, inserts the rammer, and holds it with the head against the cartridge, the staff in the axis of the piece.

4. Ram.

47. No. 1 presses firmly upon the cartridge; throws out the rammer, and places it upon the props; sweeps, if necessary, his side of the platform; passes the broom to the left side of the piece; and resumes his post.

No. 2 introduces the shell, and shoves it home in a manner similar to that prescribed for the cartridge; withdraws the hooks, and looks to see that the fuze is in the axis of the piece.

If the piece is to be fired horizontally, or at an angle of depression, No. 4, having replaced the wiper, hands a splint to No. 2, and resumes his post.

No. 2 presses the splint under the shell with the left hand; replaces the tongs and broom; and resumes his post.

The gunner pricks, leaving the priming-wire in the vent, and resumes his post.

5. In Battery.

48. Nos. 1 and 2 unchock the wheels, and with Nos. 3 and 4, all facing towards the epaulment, embar: Nos. 1 and 2 through the front spokes of the wheels, near the felly, under and perpendicularly to the cheeks; and Nos. 3 and 4 under the rear of the wheels.

The gunner, seizing his handspike, embars under the manœuvring bolts; gives the command HEAVE; and guides the piece to the middle of the embrasure; as soon as the wheels touch the hurter, he commands HALT. All unbar, and resume their posts.

6. Point.

49. Nos. 1 and 4 embar under and perpendicularly to the trail, near the manœuvring bolts.

No. 2, facing towards the epaulment, embars under the breech or knob of the cascable.

No. 3 lays down his handspike; passes the hook of the lanyard through the eye of a tube from front to rear; and holds the handle of the lanyard with the right hand, the hook between the thumb and forefinger.

The gunner, placing himself at the stock, as at the command LOAD, withdraws the priming-wire, and, aided by Nos. 1 and 4, gives the direction; causing the trail to be moved by commanding LEFT, or RIGHT, tapping, at the same time on the right side of the breech for No. 1 to move the trail to the left, or on the left side of No. 4 to move it to the right.

He then places the centre point of the breech-sight accurately upon the chalk mark on the base-ring, and commands LOWER, or RAISE, tapping, at the same time, on the upper side of the knob of the cascable with the left hand, and drawing out the quoin with the right, in order to elevate, or tapping upwards on the lower side, and shoving in the quoin, in order to depress the piece; rectifying the direction, if necessary.

If the piece is to be fired point-blank, horizontally, or at an angle of depression, he does not apply the breech-sight.

If the piece is masked from the object fired at, he places himself astride the stock, or in rear of the trail, and gives the direction by the plummet.

To give the elevation when the piece is masked, or when the desired range is greater than the breech-sight ranges, he applies the quadrant to the upper surface of the lock-piece, making the allowance due to its inclination with the axis of the piece, which ought to be previously determined.

The moment the piece is correctly pointed, he rises on the left leg, and gives the word READY, making a signal with both hands, at which Nos. 1, 2, and 4 unbar, and resume their posts; takes the breech-sight with the left hand, and goes to the windward to observe the effect of the shot.

No. 3 inserts the tube in the vent; drops the handle, allowing the lanyard to uncoil as he steps back to his post, holding it slightly stretched with the right hand, the cord passing between the fingers, back of the hand up; and breaks to the rear a full pace with the left foot, the left hand against the thigh.

Nos. 1 and 2, on resuming their posts, break off with the feet furthest from the epaulment, inclining well to that side in order to avoid the blast.

7. *Number one* (or the like)—FIRE.

50. Executed as in No. 25, except that the wheels are not chocked.

What is prescribed in No. 26 will apply to this piece.

51. To continue the exercise, the instructor resumes the series of commands, beginning with FROM BATTERY.

TO UNLOAD.

52. The piece having been run from battery, the instructor directs No. 2 to take out the shell and cartridge; No. 4 carrying them to their place in rear of the piece. No. 3 assists No. 2, by raising the breech until the shell rolls to the muzzle.

TO SCRAPE THE PIECE.

53. In the course of firing, it may become necessary to scrape the piece. To cause this to be done, the instructor directs the piece to be moved from battery, and then commands:

SCRAPE THE PIECE.

Nos. 1 and 2 lay down their handspikes.

No. 2 takes the scraper and wiper, giving the latter to No. 1; thoroughly scrapes the chamber and bore; draws out the scrapings with the spoon; returns the scraper to its place, and resumes his post.

No. 1, enveloping the sponge-head in the wiper, wipes out the bore and returns the wiper to No. 2, who replaces it; puts the sponge upon the props, and resumes his post.

To change posts.
To load for action.
To cease firing.

To secure piece, and replace implements.
To leave the battery.

Executed as in Nos. 28, 29, 31, and 32; No. 4 assisting No. 2 to take off the sleeves.

TO SERVE THE PIECE WITH REDUCED NUMBERS.

Executed as in No. 34.

TRANSPORTATION.

54. The transportation of an 8-inch siege howitzer requires eight horses and four drivers.

CHARGES, ETC.

55.

Greatest charge of powder,	4 lbs.
Greatest charge, shell filled with bullets,	3 lbs.
Charge of the shell filled with powder,	2 lbs. 9 oz.
Charge to blow out the fuze,	4 oz.
Bursting charge of the shell,	1 lb.
Greatest elevation the carriage admits,	15°
Greatest depression the carriage admits,	10°
Range at an angle of 1°, charge 4 lbs.,	430 yards.
Range at an angle of 5°, charge 4 lbs.	1150 "
Range at an angle 15°, charge 4 lbs.,	2300 "
Proof range of powder,	300 "
Weight of shell,	45 lbs.
Weight of the shell filled with bullets,	65 lbs.
The *black* fuze burns to the inch,	2 lbs.
The *red* fuze burns to the inch,	3 lbs.
The *green* fuze burns to the inch,	4 lbs.
The *yellow* fuze burns to the inch,	5 lbs.

At 2° elevation,	black fuze, full charge	The shell bursts at	500 to 600 yds.
At 3° 25′ "	red fuze, "		800 to 900 yds.
At 4° 25′ "	green fuze, "		900 to 1000 yds.
At 5° 25′ "	yellow, "		1000 to 1100 yds.

A proper charge for enfilading, at the distance of 600 yards, on a horizontal plane, relief of the epaulment seven feet, elevation 2°.75, red fuze, is three pounds.

TO PREPARE AMMUNITION.

56. If the ammunition for howitzers is to be prepared and issued by the artillery, two men, numbered 5 and 6, are added to each de-

tachment for that purpose. They are sent to the magazine, where they are provided with the following implements and stores:

1 *Set of Powder Measures.*
1 *Funnel.*
1 *Fuze-mallet.*
1 *Fuze-setter.*
1 *Fuze plug-reamer.*
1 *Rasp.*
1 *Basket.* Containing fuze-plug.
2 *Grummet-wads, or* ⎱ On which to place the shells while putting
2 *Hollow-blocks.* ⎰ in the charge.
1 *Budge-barrel.*
1 *Dark Lantern.*
Tow. For stoppers.
Cartridge bags. Of bombazine.
Twine.
Powder.
Musket bullets.
Incendiary composition.

They first fill and tie a number of cartridges, according to the directions received from the battery, and then prepare a corresponding number of shells.

To fill the cartridges. One holds the bag, while the other (by means of the funnel) pours in the powder. The cartridges thus filled are placed upright in a box until tied, when they are transported to the budge-barrel.

Cartridges of reduced charges for ricochet firing may be made thus: The charge having been poured into the bag, a wad of hay about six inches in length is placed upon it. This wad is made by laying wisps of hay evenly together, so as to form a cylinder nearly of the diameter of the cartridge bag. The wad is tied about an inch from each end, and the ends are cut squarely off, so as to present an even surface to the powder. In handling these cartridges, the powder end of the bag should always be kept downwards.

To prepare the shells. No. 5 places one upon a grummet-wad; cleanses it, if necessary, with a rasp; drives in a fuze-plug until it does not project more than the tenth of an inch; and reams it out with the reamer. No. 6, transferring it to the other grummet-wad, charges it with powder; puts in a stopper of tow; marks it with chalk; and places it conveniently for No. 4.

If the shell is to be loaded with bullets or incendiary composition, it is charged before the fuze-plug is driven. It should contain about about three hundred and twenty bullets and one pound and a quarter of powder.

If filled only with powder, No. 6 marks the shell with a cross; if with incendiary composition, he makes a circle around the fuze-plug; and if with bullets, he makes two circles on one side. The shells thus differently charged are kept separate.

LESSON III.

Service of a 10-inch Siege Mortar.

Five men are necessary; one gunner and four other cannoneers.
57. The mortar is upon its platform.
The implements, etc., are arranged as follows:

HANDSPIKES,	Two on each side of the bed against the cheeks, leaning upon the four manœuvring bolts, the small ends towards the epaulment, those of the front handspikes even with the front of the cheeks.
HAVERSACK,	Containing fuzes and a pair of sleeves. Attached to the tompion, and lying upon the mortar.
TUBE-POUCH,	Containing the priming-wire, friction tubes, and the lanyard, wound in St. Andrew's cross upon its handle. Attached to the tompion, and lying upon the mortar.
GUNNER'S-POUCH,	Containing the gunner's level, gimlet, vent-punch, and chalk. Attached to the tompion, and lying upon the mortar.
QUADRANT, PLUMMET, POINTING-CORD, SCRAPER, WIPER, SHELL-HOOKS,	In a basket between the cheeks of the mortar bed.
TOMPION,	In the muzzle.
QUOIN,	Under the mortar upon the bolster, its handle to the left.
POINTING-STAKES, MAUL, BROOM,	With the basket.

When several mortars are served together, there will be only one gunner's level, and two vent-punches to each battery, not exceeding six pieces. To the same battery there will be one *hammer-wrench*.

One shell and one paper cartridge bag for instruction, are at the magazine or other safe place in rear of the piece.

58. The cannoneers having-been marched to their posts, the instructor directs them to place their muskets against the epaulment, and explains to them the names and uses of the implements, and the nomenclatures of the mortar, its bed, and the battery.

59. To cause the pointing-stakes to be established in position, the instructor commands:

Plant the Pointing-stakes.

The gunner, assisted by Nos. 1 and 2, plants the stakes.

No. 1, having driven the pointing-stakes, drives another stake one yard behind his post for holding the wiper, and replaces the maul near the basket.

The gunner lays the slack of the pointing-cord at the foot of the epaulment, leaving the plummet at the stake in the rear of the piece.

All resume their posts.

60. To cause the implements to be distributed, the instructor commands:

Take Implements.

The gunner steps to the front of the piece; gives to No. 1 the sleeves and the wiper; to No. 2 the basket and maul; to No. 3 the tube-pouch and broom; and to No. 4 the haversack; equips himself with the gunner's pouch; applies his level to ascertain the line of metal, which he marks with chalk; and resumes his post.

No. 1 places the wiper upon the stake behind him, and, assisted by No. 3, puts on the sleeves.

No. 2 removes the tompion, which he places with the basket and maul, one yard behind him, and lays the shell-hooks on the ground between himself and the basket.

No. 3 lays the broom on the ground behind him, and equips himself with the tube-pouch.

No. 4 equips himself with the haversack, which he wears from the right shoulder to the left side.

All take their handspikes.

61. The handspikes are held as in No. 16. When laid down, they are returned, except in one case, to their places on the manœuvring bolt.

62. The instructor causes the service of the piece to be executed by the following commands:

1. IN BATTERY.

The gunner, making a half-face to his right, steps off, left foot first, and places himself two paces in rear of the platform, facing the piece.

Nos. 1, 2, 3, and 4, facing towards the epaulment, embar: Nos. 1 and 2 under the front manœuvring bolts, and Nos. 3 and 4 under those in the rear, engaging the butts of their handspikes about three inches.

All being ready, the gunner gives the command, HEAVE, which will be repeated as often as may be necessary. As soon as the piece is on the middle of the platform, he commands HALT. All unbar, and resume their posts.

2. *Load by Detail*—LOAD.

63. Nos. 1, 3, and 4, lay down their handspikes.

The gunner taking the scraper, places himself in front of the muzzle, and scrapes the bore and chamber; draws out the scrapings with the spoon; returns the scraper to the basket, and again places himself at the muzzle, one yard in its front.

No. 1, turning to his right, takes the wiper with the right hand; faces to his left, and places the left foot near the manœuvring bolt, the right in front of the muzzle, the left hand upon the face of the piece; thoroughly wipes out the chamber and bore, and resumes his post.

No. 3, as soon as the piece is wiped, clears the vent with the priming-wire; sweeps the platform, if necessary, and resumes his post and handspike.

Nos. 2 and 4, facing to their right—No. 2 holding his handspike at the middle under the left arm, butt end foremost, and taking the shell-hooks in the right—go to the rear for a cartridge and shell. While No. 4 is getting the cartridge, No. 2 inserts the shell-hooks in the ears of the shell, and passes the small end of the handspike through the ring. In carrying the shell they hold the handspike with their right hands, No. 4 at the small end and in advance of

No. 2. Passing by the left of the piece, between the gunner and the muzzle, they rest the shell upon the platform against the middle of the transom.

No. 1, placing the wiper upon the handspike, receives the small end of the handspike from No. 4, who gives the cartridge to the gunner.

The gunner advances the left foot, and places the left hand upon the face of the piece; introduces the cartridge into the mouth of the chamber with the right hand, and carefully pours in the powder; returns the cartridge bag to No. 4, and distributes the powder evenly over the bottom of the chamber. In firing with paper fuzes, he receives one from No. 4, and inserts it in the fuze-plug.

No. 4, returning the cartridge bag to the haversack, takes the wiper.

Nos. 1 and 2 raise the shell and hold it about a foot from the ground, while No. 4 wipes it; they then lift it into the muzzle.

The gunner steps forward, and with the left hand over the handspike, the right hand under and nearer to it, seizes the shell-hooks and assists to lower the shell gently into its place. No. 2 then withdraws his handspike from the ring, and resumes his post. No. 1 takes his handspike. The gunner adjusts the shell so that the fuze is in the axis of the piece; throws the shell hooks to their place behind No. 2; and, if firing with wooden fuzes, uncaps the fuze.

No. 4, as soon as he wipes the shell, returns the wiper to its place; takes the slack of the pointing-cord, which he lays over the left manœuvring bolts, leaving its end at the rear pointing-stake; and resumes his post and handspike.

3. POINT.

64. Nos. 1 and 2, facing towards the epaulment, embar upon the bolster, under and perpendicularly to the piece.

The gunner taking the quadrant from the basket, applies it to the left side of the face of the piece with the left hand, and inserts or draws out the quoin with the right, giving the command RAISE, or LOWER, until the piece is at the elevation required—usually 45°. Returning the quadrant to the basket—Nos. 1 and 2 at the same time unbarring and resuming their posts—he places himself in rear of the rear pointing-stake, and holding the pointing-cord in the left hand and the plummet in the right, gives the direction; commanding MORTAR LEFT, MORTAR RIGHT; MUZZLE LEFT, MUZZLE RIGHT; TRAIL LEFT, TRAIL RIGHT, as may be required.

To throw the mortar to the left. Nos. 2 and 4, facing each other, embar under the manœuvring bolts. Nos. 1 and 3, facing towards the epaulment, embar under the notches near them. When all are ready, the gunner gives the command, HEAVE STEADY. The cannoneers remain embarred until he gives some other command, or makes the signal to unbar.

To throw the mortar to the right. Nos. 1 and 3 embar under the manœuvring bolts. Nos. 2 and 4 embar under the notches.

To throw the muzzle to the left. Nos. 1 and 3, facing towards the epaulment, embar under the front notches; No. 1 under the inside of the left notch.

To throw the trail to the left.—Nos. 1 and 3, facing towards the epaulment, embar under the rear notches; No. 3 under the inside of the left notch.

The muzzle or trail is thrown to the right, in a similar manner to the preceding, by Nos. 2 and 4.

The direction having been given, the gunner gives the word, READY, and makes a signal with both hands; leaves the plummet at the stake; returns the pointing-cord to the foot of the epaulment; and goes to the windward to observe the effect of the shot.

Nos. 1, 2, and 4, taking their handspikes with them, go four yards in rear of the platform, and face to the front; No. 4 between Nos. 1 and 2, their handspikes held erect by the right side, the right arm extended naturally.

No. 3 lays down his handspike six inches in his front, parallel to the edge of the platform, and makes ready a friction tube, as in No. 24; advancing the right foot, he puts the tube in the vent; rises on the left leg, and moves three paces to the rear in prolongation of the right cheek; faces to the front; holds the handle of the lanyard with the right hand, the lanyard slightly stretched, the cord passing between the fingers, back of the hand up; and breaks to the rear a full pace with the left foot, the left hand against the thigh.

Remark.—To discharge the mortars now in use by means of a friction tube, the lanyard should be passed under a rope attached to and tightly drawn between the rear manœuvring bolts, or through a loop of rope attached to the rear right manœuvring bolt.

4. *Number one* (or the like)—FIRE.

65. Executed as in No. 25.

On the discharge of the piece, all resume their posts except the gunner, who waits to observe the effect of the shot. As soon as the shot strikes he resumes his post.

What is prescribed in No. 26 will apply to this piece, omitting the word "*lock*."

66. To continue the exercise, the instructor causes the piece to be moved towards the rear of the platform, directs Nos. 2 and 4 to take out the shell and carry it to the rear, and then resumes the series of commands beginning with In Battery.

TO CHANGE POSTS. TO LOAD FOR ACTION. TO CEASE FIRING.

Executed as in Nos. 28, 29, and 30, except that in changing posts No. 2 passes by the front of the piece.

TO SECURE PIECE, AND REPLACE IMPLEMENTS.

67. To discontinue the exercise, the instructor having ordered the firing to cease, and caused the piece to be placed as at the command, IN BATTERY, gives the command:

REPLACE IMPLEMENTS.

All lay down their handspikes. No. 2 puts in the tompion, and assists No. 1 to pull up the pointing-stakes. The gunner receives the implements from the cannoneers, and replaces them between the cheeks.

TO LEAVE THE BATTERY.

Executed as in No. 32.

TRANSPORTATION.

68. One mortar wagon is allowed to each 10-inch siege mortar and bed; to transport which requires eight horses and four drivers.

CHARGES, ETC.

69.

Greatest charge of powder,	4 lbs.
Ordinary service charge,	3 "
Charge of the shell filled with powder	5 "
Bursting charge of the shell,	2 "
Charge to blow out the fuse,	5 oz.
Range, charge 4 lbs., time of flight 21″,	2100 yards.
Range, charge 3 lbs., time of flight 19″,	1700 "
Range, charge 2 lbs., time of flight 14″,	1000 "
Proof range of powder,	300 "
Weight of the shell,	90 lbs.

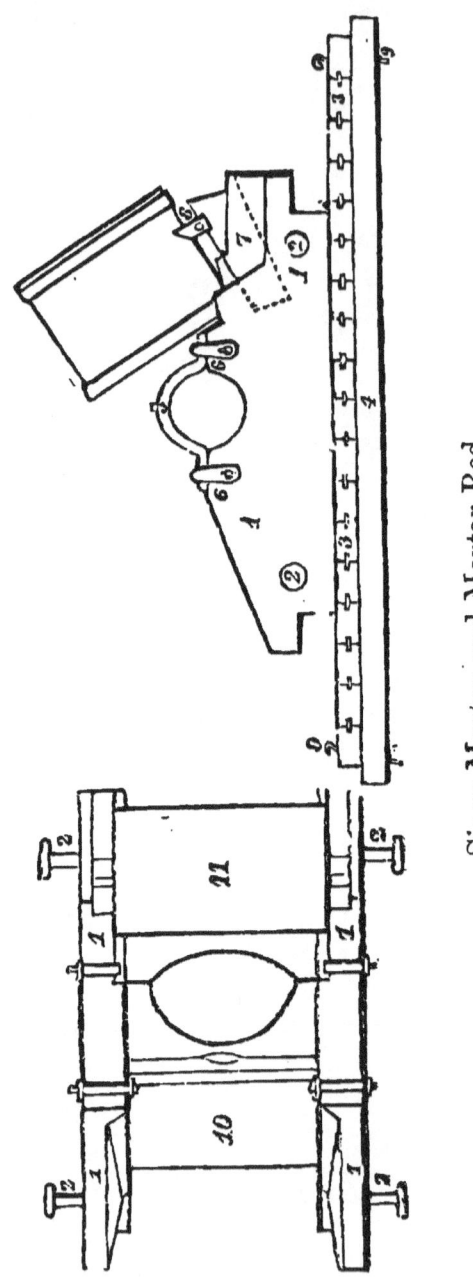

Siege Mortar and Mortar Bed.

1. Cheeks,
2. Manœuvring Bolts,
3. Deck Plank,
4. Sleeper,
5. Cap Square,
6. " Straps,
7. Bolster,
8. Quoin,
9. Eye Bolts,
10. Middle Transom,
11. Front Transom.

Five balls, according to their size, are fired from mortars of corresponding calibres. With a charge of *one-twenty-fifth* of its weight the ball is thrown from six hundred to seven hundred yards.

TO PREPARE AMMUNITION.

70. If the ammunition for mortars is to be prepared and issued by the artillery, two men, numbered 5 and 6, are added to each detachment for that purpose. Their duties at the magazine are similar to those prescribed in No. 56.

Should wooden fuses be used, in addition to the implements therein mentioned, a *fuze-saw* will be required for reducing the fuzes to the proper lengths. The shell being first charged, the fuze, cut at the right length, is then driven.

The paper fuze is marked with the number of seconds which it burns per inch. It may be cut with a knife to any desired length.

TIME OF FLIGHT.

71. The time of flight for siege mortars, at an elevation of 45°, with ordinary charges, is nearly equal to the square root of the range in feet divided by four.

The experimental length of the fuze may be given according to this rule.

TO ASCERTAIN THE DISTANCE BY THE REPORT OF FIRE-ARMS.

72. Multiply the number of seconds which elapse between seeing the flash and hearing the report by 1,100; the product will be nearly the distance in feet.

RAPIDITY OF FIRING.

73. Siege mortars can be fired conveniently at the rate of twelve rounds an hour continuously; but they may in case of need, be fired with greater rapidity.

LESSON IV.

Service of an 8-inch Siege Mortar.

Three men are necessary: one gunner and two other cannoneers.
74. The mortar is upon its platform.

The implements. etc., omitting two handspikes, and adding one grummet-wad, are the same as prescribed for the 10-inch siege mortar in No. 57. They are arranged as prescribed in that number. The wad is in the basket.

75. The instruction for this piece is the same as that prescribed in Lesson III, with the following modifications:

At the command TAKE IMPLEMENTS, No. 1 performs the duties enjoined on No. 3, and No. 2 those of No. 4, each in addition to his own. No. 2 assists No. 1 to put on the sleeves, and places the wad on the platform in front of the transom.

76. At the command IN BATTERY, No. 1 embars under the right front manœuvring bolts. No. 2 embars under the left rear manœuvring bolts.

77. At the command LOAD, No. 1, having wiped out the mortar, places the wiper upon the stake; pricks; and, if necessary, sweeps the platform.

No. 2, laying down his handspike, goes for a cartridge and shell; carries the shell in the right arm; passes between the gunner and the muzzle, and places it on the wad; gives to the gunner the cartridge, and if firing with paper fuzes, a fuze; and takes the wiper from the stake.

The gunner, on returning the scraper to the basket, takes the shell-hooks and lays them on the ground between himself and the muzzle. Having carefully poured in the powder, he returns the cartridge-bag to No. 2, and distributes the powder evenly over the bottom of the chamber; puts the fuze in the fuze-plug; inserts the hooks in the ears of the shell; raises it about a foot from the ground and holds it, while No. 2 wipes it; and then places it in the bore.

No. 2 replaces the wiper upon the stake; lays the slack of the pointing-cord over the left manœuvring bolts; and resumes his post.

78. At the command POINT, Nos. 1 and 2 embar under either of the front or rear notches, as required. At the signal from the gunner, No. 1 prepares to fire the piece, as prescribed for No. 3, in No. 64.

TRANSPORTATION.

79. One mortar wagon will carry three 8-inch siege mortars, with their beds; to transport which requires eight horses and four drivers.

CHARGES, ETC.

80.

Greatest charge of powder,	2 lbs.
Ordinary service charge,	1 lb. 12 oz.
Charge of the shell filled with powder,	2 lbs. 9 oz.
Bursting charge of the shell,	1 lb.
Charge to blow out the fuze,	4 oz.
Range, charge 2 lbs., time of flight 20″,	1,837 yards.
Range, charge 1¼ lb., time of flight 14″,	943 yards.
Proof range of powder,	300 yards.
Weight of shell,	45 lbs.

LESSON V.

Service of a Coehorn Mortar.

Three men are necessary: one gunner and two other cannoneers.

81. The mortar is upon its platform.

The implements, etc., and their arrangement, are the same as prescribed for the 8-inch siege mortar in No. 74. A 24-pdr. shell is used.

82. The instruction for this piece is the same as that prescribed in Lesson IV.

To prepare its ammunition, and to transport it by hand with ease, two additional men are required. The gunner carries the basket and implements.

83. It is fired either from behind intrenchments, like other mortars, or it may accompany troops in effecting lodgments in towns and fortified places.

84. As the shell is without ears, it should be strapped with tin, having loops attached, through which a cord is passed for the purpose of lowering it into the bore. The chamber being cylindrical, a sponge is used, which is handled by No. 1.

CHARGES, ETC.

85.

Greatest charge of powder,	8 oz.
Charge of the shell filled with powder,	1 lb.
Bursting charge of the shell,	8 oz.

Charge to blow out the fuze, - - - - - 2 oz.
Range, charge 8 oz., - - - - - 1,200 yards
Range, charge 6 oz., - - - - - 900 "
Range, charge 4 oz., - - - - - 430 "
Proof range of powder, - - - - - 300 "
Weight of shell, - - - - - 17 lbs.

LESSON VI.

Service of a 10-inch Sea-coast Mortar.

Five men are necessary: one gunner and four other cannoneers.
86. The mortar is upon its platform.

The implements, etc., with the addition of one sponge, are the same as prescribed for the 10-inch siege mortar in No. 57. They are arranged as prescribed in that number, except that the sponge is placed upon props one yard behind No. 1, the sponge-head turned towards the epaulment.

87. The instruction for this piece is the same as that prescribed in Lesson III, with the following modifications:

No. 1, after wiping the bore, sponges out the chamber; for this purpose mounting upon the right cheek and bolster.

To scrape the bore, and to put in the cartridge and shell, the gunner mounts upon a block in front of the muzzle.

The cartridge—its bag being of bombazine or flannel—is put directly into the chamber by the gunner, and rammed by No. 1.

To lift the shell into the muzzle, Nos. 2 and 3 mount the cheeks, and are assisted respectively by the gunner and No. 1.

In giving the elevation, Nos. 1 and 2 are assisted by Nos. 3 and 4.

Before priming, No. 3 pricks a second time.

CHARGES, ETC.

88.
Greatest charge of powder, - - - - - 10 lbs.
Charge of shell filled with powder, - - - - - 5 "
Bursting charge of the shell, - - - - - 2 "
Charge to blow out the fuze, - - - - - 5 oz.
Range, charge 10 lbs., time of flight 36″, - - - 4,250 yards.
Proof range of powder, - - - - - 300 "
Weight of shell, - - - - - 90 lbs.

LESSON VII.

Service of a 13-inch Sea-coast Mortar.

Five men are necessary: one gunner and four other cannoneers.
89. The mortar is upon its platform.
The implements, etc., and their arrangement, are the same as prescribed for the 10-inch sea-coast mortar in No. 86.
90. The instruction for this piece differs in no respect from that prescribed in Lesson VI.

CHARGES, ETC.

91.

Greatest charge of powder,	20 lbs.
Charge of the shell filled with powder,	11 "
Bursting charge of the shell,	6 "
Charge to blow out the fuze,	6 oz.
Range, charge 20 lbs., time of flight (about) 40″,	4,325 yards.
Proof range of powder,	300 "
Weight of shell,	200 lbs.

LESSON VIII.

Service of a Stone Mortar.

Five men are necessary: one gunner and four other cannoneers.
92. The mortar is upon its platform.
The implements, etc., and their arrangement, are the same as prescribed for the 10-inch sea-coast mortar in No. 86.
93. The instruction for this piece differs in no respect from that prescribed in Lesson VI.
A wooden bottom is placed over the mouth of the chamber to receive the basket which contains the charge of stones.

CHARGES, ETC.

94. With a charge of a pound and a half of powder, and one hundred and twenty pounds of stones, at an elevation of 60°, the stones are thrown from one hundred and fifty to two hundred and fifty yards.

5

With fifteen 6-pdr. shells, fuze fifteen seconds, charge of powder one pound, elevation 33°, the shell may be thrown from fifty to one hundred and fifty yards.

95. As the shells are liable to burst on leaving the bore, the piece is fired by a slow match applied to a train of quick match, giving the men time to place themselves under cover.

LESSON IX.

Service of a Gun mounted on a Barbette Carriage.

Remark.—The instruction for a barbette gun, although in many respects precisely the same as that for a siege gun, is given in full, because the siege gun is seldom found in the forts on the sea-board.

Five men are necessary: one gunner and four other cannoneers.
96. The piece is in battery.
The implements, etc., are arranged as follows:

HANDSPIKES,	Two on each side of the carriage leaning against the parapet, in line with the cannoneers.
SPONGE RAMMER,	One yard behind the cannoneers of the right, the sponge uppermost, the sponge and rammer-heads turned from the parapet, inclined slightly from the piece, and supported upon a prop; or, when this cannot be done conveniently, placed against the wall, the sponge and rammer-heads nearest the piece.
PASS-BOX,	Against the parapet, outside of the pile of balls.
TUBE-POUCH,	Containing friction tubes, and the lanyard, wound in St. Andrew's cross upon its handle. Suspended from the knob of the cascable.
GUNNER'S-POUCH,	Containing the gunner's level, breech sight, finger-stall, priming-wire, gimlet, vent-punch, chalk-line, and chalk. Suspended from the knob of the cascable.
CHOCKS,	One on each side of the piece, at the foot of the parapet, inside the handspikes.
VENT-COVER.	Covering the vent.

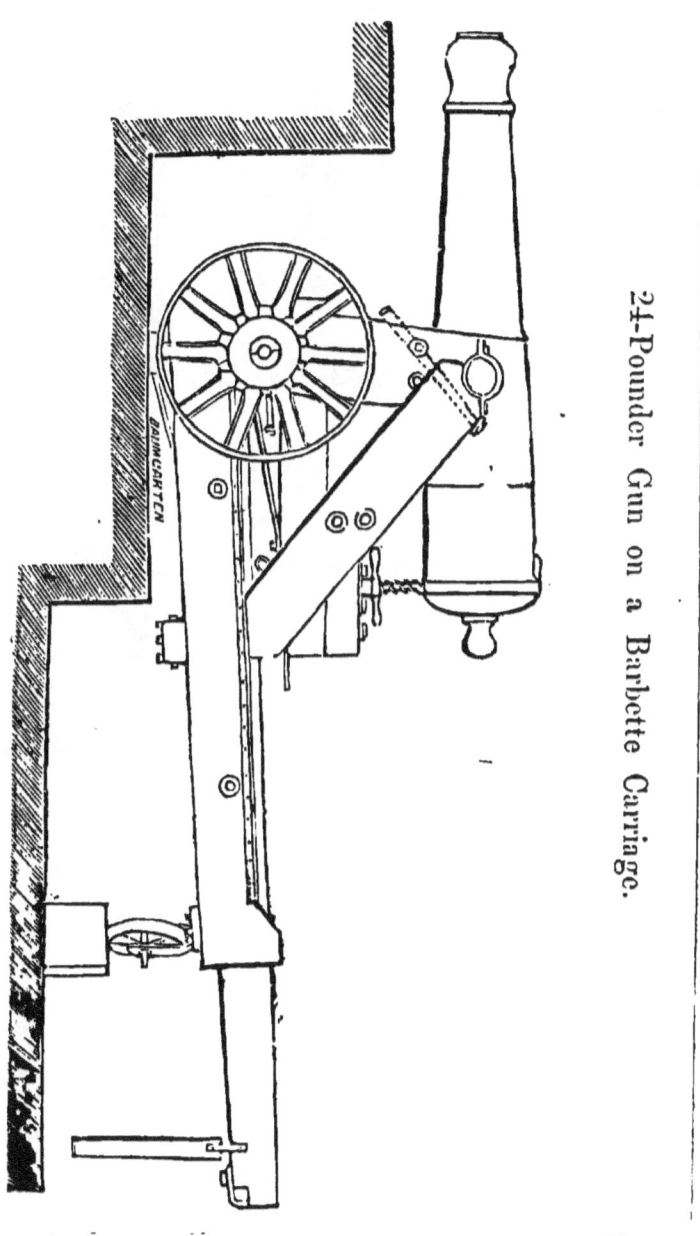

24-Pounder Gun on a Barbette Carriage.

TOMPION,	. . .	In the muzzle.
BROOM,	. . .	{ Leaning against the parapet, outside of the pile of balls.
BUDGE-BARREL,		{ Containing cartridges, at the safest and most convenient place in rear of the piece.

When several guns are served together, there will be only one gunner's level and two vent-punches to each battery, not exceeding six pieces. To the same battery there will be one *worm*, one *ladle*, and one *wrench*.

The balls are regularly piled on the banquette, on the left of the piece.

The wads are placed between the parapet and the balls, partly resting on them.

97. The cannoneers having been marched to their posts, the instructor explains to them the names and uses of the implements, and the nomenclatures of the gun, its carriage and the battery.

98. To cause the implements to be distributed, the instructor commands:

Take Implements.

The gunner mounts upon the tongue; takes off the vent-cover, handing it to No. 2 to place against the parapet, outside of the pass-box; gives the tube-pouch to No. 3; equips himself with his own pouch and the finger-stall, wearing the latter on the second finger of the left hand; levels the piece by the elevating screw; applies his level to ascertain the line of metal, which, with the assistance of No. 2, he marks with the chalk-line; and resumes his post.

No. 3 equips himself with the tube-pouch.

Nos. 1 and 2, after passing handspikes to Nos. 3 and 4, take each one for himself.

99. The handspike is held in both hands; the hand nearest to the parapet grasping it near the small end and at the height of the shoulder, back of the hand down, elbow touching the body: the other hand back up, the arm extended naturally; the butt of the handspike upon the ground on the side farthest from the parapet, and six inches in advance of the alignment.

100. When the cannoneer lays down his handspike, he places it directly before him, about six inches in advance of and parallel to the alignment, the small end towards the parapet; and whenever he thus lays it down for the performance of any particular duty,

he will resume it on returning to his post after the completion of that duty.

101. The instructor causes the service of the piece to be executed by the following commands:

1. FROM BATTERY.

The gunner moves two paces to his right.

Nos. 1, 2, 3, and 4, facing from the parapet, embar, near the tire; Nos. 1 and 2 first facing the chocks on the rails in front of the rollers through the front spokes of the wheels, over the front manœuvring bolts; and Nos. 3 and 4 through the rear spokes, under the rear manœuvring bolts.

Should there be no rear manœuvring bolts, Nos 3 and 4 embar under the braces, near the manœuvring staples.

All being ready, the gunner gives the command HEAVE, which will be repeated as often as may be necessary. As soon as the face of the piece is about one yard from the parapet, he commands HALT. All unbar, and resume their posts. Nos. 1 and 2 chock the rollers.

2. *Load by Detail*—LOAD.

102. Nos. 1, 2, 3 and 4 lay down their handspikes.

No. 2 takes out the tompion, and places it near the vent-cover.

No. 1 faces once and a half to his left; steps over the sponge and rammer; faces the piece; takes the sponge with both hands, the backs-down, the right hand three feet from the sponge-head, the left hand eighteen inches nearer to it; returns to the piece, placing the left foot on the rail of the chassis in line with the face of the piece, the right in the most convenient position; and rests the end of the sponge in the muzzle, the staff in the prolongation of the bore, supported by the right hand, the right arm extended, the left hand flat against the side of the thigh.

Remark.—In order that Nos. 1 and 2 may load with facility without standing on the chassis, a banquette should be placed between the head of the chassis and the wall, or a platform attached to the head of the chassis.

No. 2 steps upon the rail on his side, and occupies a position on the left of the piece corresponding to that of No. 1 on its right. He seizes the staff with the left hand, back down, near to and outside of the hand of No. 1.

MANUAL FOR HEAVY ARTILLERY. 101

No. 3, as soon as the sponge is inserted in the bore, steps over the rammer, and seizes the staff with both hands, as prescribed for the sponge; returns to his post; and stands ready to exchange with No. 1.

No. 4 takes the pass-box and goes to the rear for a cartridge; returns with it, and places himself, facing the piece, about eighteen inches to the rear and right of No. 2.

The gunner mounts upon the tongue of the chassis, placing the left foot about six inches from the rear transom of the gun carriage, and breaks well to the rear with the right foot, the toe to the right; closes the vent with the second finger of the left hand, bending well forward to cover himself by the breech; and turns the elevating screw with the right hand, so as to adjust the piece conveniently for loading.

103. In the mean time Nos. 1 and 2 insert the sponge by the following motions:

First motion.—They insert the sponge as far as the hand of No. 1, bodies erect, shoulders square.

Second motion.—They slide the hands along the staff, and seize it at arm's length.

Third motion.—They force the sponge down as prescribed in the first motion.

Fourth motion.—They repeat the second motion.

Fifth motion.—They push the sponge to the bottom of the bore. No. 1. replaces the left hand on the staff, back up, six inches nearer to the muzzle than the right. No. 2 places the right hand, back up, between the hands of No. 1.

If in executing these motions, or the corresponding ones with the rammer, it be found that the sponge or rammer is at home at the third or fourth motion, then what is prescribed for the fifth motion will be performed at the third or fourth. The knee on the side towards which the body is to be inclined is always bent, the other straightened; and the weight of the body added, as much as possible, to the effort exerted by the arms.

3. Sponge.

104. Nos. 1 and 2, pressing the sponge firmly against the bottom of the bore, turn it three times from right to left, and three times from left to right; replace the hands on the thighs; and withdraw the sponge by motions contrary to those prescribed for inserting it.

Remark.—To handle the sponge when it is new and fits tight, it may become necessary for Nos. 1 and 2 to use both hands. In this case it will be inserted and withdrawn by short and quick motions.

No. 2 quits the staff, and turning towards No. 4, receives from him the cartridge, which he takes in both hands, back down, and introduces into the bore bottom foremost, seams to the sides; he then grasps the rammer in the way prescribed for the sponge.

No. 1, rising upon the right leg and turning towards his left, passes the sponge above the rammer with the left hand to No. 3, and receiving the rammer with the right, presents it as prescribed for the sponge, except that he rests the rammer-head against the right side of the face of the piece.

No. 3, as soon as the sponge is withdrawn, passing the rammer under the sponge with the right hand, receives the sponge from No. 1 with the left, replaces it upon the prop, and resumes his post.

No. 4, setting down the pass-box, takes out the cartridge and presents it in both hands to No. 2, the choke to the front; returns the pass-box to its place, and picks up a ball, and afterwards a wad, should one be required.

Nos. 1 and 2 force down the cartridge by the motions prescribed for forcing down the sponge.

4. Ram.

105. Nos. 1 and 2, drawing the rammer out to the full extent of their arms, ram with a single stroke. No. 2 quits the staff, and turning towards No. 4, receives from him the ball and wad, while No. 1 throws out the rammer, and holds the head against the right side of the face of the piece. No. 2, receiving successively the ball and wad, introduces them into the bore, the ball first, and seizes the staff with the left hand. No. 4 then resumes his post.

Nos. 1 and 2 force down the ball and wad together by the same motions, and ram in the same manner as prescribed for the cartridge. No. 2 quits the rammer; sweeps, if necessary, the platform on his own side; passes the broom to No. 1; and resumes his post. No. 1 throws out the rammer, and places it upon the prop below the sponge; finishes the sweeping; and resumes his post.

The gunner pricks, leaving the priming-wire in the vent, and, if firing beyond point-blank range, adjusts the breech-sight to the distance.

5. IN BATTERY.

106. Nos. 1 and 2 unchock the rollers, and with Nos. 3 and 4, all facing towards the parapet, embar; Nos. 1 and 2 through the front spokes of the wheels, near the tire, under the manœuvring bolts; and Nos. 3 and 4 under the braces, near the manœuvring staples.

All being ready, the gunner commands HEAVE, and the piece is run into battery; the gunner following up the movement. As soon as the rollers touch the hurters, he commands HALT. All unbar, and Nos. 1, 2, 3, and 4 resume their posts.

6. POINT.

107. No. 3 lays down his handspike, passes the hook of the lanyard through the eye of a tube from front to rear, and holds the handle of the lanyard with the right hand, the hook between the thumb and forefinger.

Nos. 1 and 4 go to the traverse wheels, and, facing towards the parapet, embar under the fork-bolts or under the wheels. No. 1, in passing from and to his post, moves on the outside of No. 3.

The gunner withdraws the priming-wire, and, aided by Nos. 1 and 4, gives the direction; causing the trail to be moved by commanding LEFT, or RIGHT, tapping at the same time on the right side of the breech for No. 1 to move the chassis to the left, or on the left side for No. 4 to move it to the right.

He then places the centre point of the breech-sight accurately upon the chalk mark on the base-ring, and by the elevating screw gives the proper elevation, rectifying the direction, if necessary.

The moment the piece is correctly pointed, he rises on the left leg, and gives the word READY, making a signal with both hands, at which Nos. 1 and 4 unbar, and resume their posts; takes the breech-sight with the left hand, and receiving the tube from No. 3, inserts it in the vent; dismounts from the tongue; and goes to the windward to observe the effect of the shot.

No. 3 drops the handle, allowing the lanyard to uncoil as he steps back to his post, holding it slightly stretched with the right hand, the cord passing between the fingers, back of the hand up; and breaks to the rear a full pace with the left foot, the left hand against the thigh.

At the word READY, Nos. 1 and 2 take the chocks, and breaking off with the feet farthest from the parapet, stand ready to chock the rollers.

108. In directing the piece to be fired, the instructor will designate it by its number, as, for example:

7. Number one—FIRE.

No. 3 gives a smart pull upon the lanyard.

Immediately after the discharge of the piece, Nos. 1 and 2 chock the rollers, and resume the erect position. No. 3 resumes the erect position, and rewinds the lanyard in St. Andrew's cross upon its handle, returning it if dry to the tube-pouch. The gunner, having observed the effect of the shot, returns to his post.

109. Whenever the piece is to be fired by a *lock, port-fire,* or *slow-match*, it will be done by No. 3, as prescribed for No. 4, in the instruction for field artillery.

110. To continue the exercise, the instructor resumes the series of commands, beginning with FROM BATTERY.

TO CHANGE POSTS.

111. To change posts the instructor commands:

1. CHANGE POSTS. 2. MARCH. 3. CALL OFF.

At the first command, the cannoneers lay down their handspikes; place their equipments on the parts of the carriage nearest to them; and face to their left.

At the second command, they step off, each advancing one post; No. 2 taking that of No. 1. Nos. 2 and 3 pass to the rear of the chassis; No. 2 on the outside of all the cannoneers. On arriving at their posts, they face to the piece, and equip themselves.

At the third command, they call off, according to the posts they are to occupy.

TO LOAD FOR ACTION.

112. The cannoneers having been sufficiently instructed in the details of the movements, the instructor commands:

Load for action—LOAD.

The piece is run from battery, loaded, run into battery, pointed, and prepared for firing, by the following commands from the gunner: FROM BATTERY—LOAD—IN BATTERY—POINT—READY.

At the command or signal from the instructor to commence firing, the gunner gives the command FIRE, and continues the action until the instructor directs the firing to cease.

TO CEASE FIRING.

113. To cause the firing to cease, the instructor commands:

CEASE FIRING.

Whether the cannoneers are *loading by detail* or *for action*, the piece is sponged out, and all resume their posts. If the cartridge has been inserted, the loading will be completed, unless the instructor should otherwise direct.

TO SECURE PIECE, AND REPLACE IMPLEMENTS.

114. To discontinue the exercise, the instructor having ordered the firing to cease, and caused the piece to be run into battery, gives the following commands:

1. SECURE PIECE.

No. 2 returns the tompion to the muzzle, the gunner puts on the vent-cover, which he receives from No. 2, and depresses the piece.

2. REPLACE IMPLEMENTS.

Nos. 1 and 2 replace the handspikes against the parapet, Nos. 3 and 4 passing theirs to them for that purpose. The gunner hangs the pouches upon the knob of the cascable.

TO LEAVE THE BATTERY.

115. The instructor forms the detachment in rear of the piece; and marches it from the battery as prescribed in No. 12.

TO SERVE THE PIECE WITH REDUCED NUMBERS.

Executed as in No. 34.

CHARGES, ETC.

Wads.
Rapidity of firing.
Penetration of shot.
See Nos. 37, 39, and 40.

LESSON XII.

Service of a Gun mounted on a Casemate Carriage.

Five men are necessary; one gunner and four other cannoneers.
120. The piece is in battery.
The implements, etc., are arranged as follows:

TRUCK-HAND-SPIKES,	One on each side of the carriage, leaning against the wall, in line with the cannoneers.
ELEVATING-HAND-SPIKES,	One on each side of the carriage, leaning against the wall, behind Nos. 3 and 4*.
TRAVERSING-HANDSPIKES,	One on each side of the carriage, leaning against the wall, opposite to the end of the tongue.
ROLLER-HAND-SPIKE,	Leaning against the wall, behind the gunner, or laid down in the alignment on his right.
SPONGE-RAMMER,	About one yard behind the cannoneers of the right, the sponge uppermost, the sponge and rammer-heads turned from the embrasure, inclined slightly from the piece, and supported upon a proper block.
PASS-BOX,	Behind No. 4.
TUBE-POUCH,	Containing friction tubes, and the lanyard, wound in St. Andrew's cross upon its handle. Suspended from the knob of the cascable.
GUNNERS'-POUCH,	Containing the gunner's level, breech-sight, finger-stall, priming-wire, gimlet, vent-punch, and chalk-line, and chalk. Suspended from the knob of the cascable.
CHOCKS,	One on each side of the carriage, on the front transom of the chassis, handles outwards.
VENT-COVER,	Covering the vent.
TOMPION,	In the muzzle.

* These are *manœuvring* handspikes. With two pieces in one casemate, or where the pieces are not separated by piers, they may be placed against the nearest wall, or laid down in the most convenient position.

BROOM,	Leaning against the scarp-wall, on the left of the piece.
BUDGE-BARREL,	Containing cartridges, at the safest and most convenient place in rear of the piece.

When several guns are served together, there will be only one gunner's level and two vent-punches to each battery, not exceeding six pieces. To the same battery there will be one *worm*, one *ladle*, and one *wrench*.

The balls are regularly piled against the wall, behind No. 2.

The wads are placed between the wall and the balls, partly resting on them.

121. The cannoneers having been marched to their posts, the instructor explains to them the names and uses of the implements, and the nomenclatures of the gun, its carriage, and the battery.

122. To cause the implements to be distributed, the instructor commands:

TAKE IMPLEMENTS.

The gunner mounts upon the tongue; takes off the vent-cover, handing it to No. 2 to place against the scarp; gives the tube-pouch to No. 3; and equips himself with his own pouch and finger-stall, wearing the latter on the second finger of the left hand. With the assistance of No. 3 he levels the piece, and applies his level to ascertain the line of metal, which, with the assistance of No. 2, he marks with the chalk line. (If the gun has permanent sights, this is only necessary for instruction, or for verifying the sight.) He then takes the roller-handspike, and resumes his post. This handspike is held vertically with the right hand, the lower end upon the ground in line with the toes, the arms extended naturally.

No. 3 equips himself with the tube-pouch.

Nos. 1 and 2 take the truck-handspikes with the hand farthest from the wall, and carry them to that side, holding them vertically, the lower end upon the ground in line with the toes, the arms extended naturally.

123. The instructor causes the service of the piece to be executed by the following commands:

1. FROM BATTERY.

The gunner embars in the left mortise of the roller.

Nos. 1 and 2, facing from the scarp wall, embar in the most convenient front mortises of the truck-wheels, the hand farthest from the carriage at the top of the handspike, the other hand eight inches lower.

Nos. 3 and 4 go to the assistance of Nos. 1 and 2, and, facing towards them, seize the handspikes with both hands between those of Nos. 1 and 2.

Nos. 1, 2, 3, and 4 in applying themselves to the carriage either to run it from or to battery, break to the rear with the foot nearest to the carriage.

All being ready, the gunner presses the roller under the rear transom of the gun carriage, by bearing down upon his handspike, and gives the command, HEAVE.

Nos. 1, 2, 3, and 4 act together, and bear upon the handspikes until they are nearly down to the rails. The gunner then disengages the roller from under the transom by raising his handspike, and commands, UNBAR. Nos. 1 and 2 let go the handspikes with the hand nearest to the carriage, and chock the wheels. Nos. 3 and 4 withdraw the handspikes and pass them to Nos. 1 and 2, who reinsert them in the front mortises.

The gunner again bearing down upon his handspike, gives the command, HEAVE, and so on, until the face of the piece is about one yard from the wall, when, raising his handspike, he commands, HALT, and shifts it into the right mortise of the roller. Nos. 1 and 2 chock the wheels, and replace their handspikes against the wall. All resume their posts.

2. *Load by detail*—LOAD.

124. Executed as in Nos. 103 and 104, with the following modification: No. 3, facing towards the scarp, embars under the breech, and maintains the piece in a convenient position for inserting the sponge, until he receives a signal from the gunner to unbar.

3. SPONGE.

125. Executed as in No. 104.

4. RAM.

126. Executed as in No. 105.

5. In Battery.

127. Nos. 1 and 2 unchock the wheels, and, facing from the scarp wall apply their hands to the front of the cheeks.

Nos. 3 and 4, facing towards the scarp wall, lay hold of the handles.

The gunner bears down carefully upon the roller-handspike, and the piece is run into battery. As soon as the wheels touch the hurters, he commands, HALT. Nos. 1, 2, 3, and 4 resume their posts.

6. Point.

128. Nos. 1 and 4 take the traversing handspikes, and, facing towards the scarp wall, embar under the ends of the rear transom of the chassis. No. 1, in passing to and from his post, moves on the outside of No. 3.

When the elevation is given by the quoin, No. 2 takes an elevating handspike and embars upon the left cheek under the reinforce.

The gunner withdraws the priming-wire, and, aided by Nos. 1 and 4, gives the direction, as in No. 107.

He then applies the breech sight, if necessary, and points the piece; commanding LOWER, or RAISE, tapping at the same time on the upper side of the knob of the cascable with the left hand, and drawing out the quoin with the right, in order to elevate, or tapping upwards on the lower side and shoving in the quoin, in order to depress the piece.

The moment the piece is correctly pointed, he rises on the left leg and gives the word, READY, making a signal with both hands, at which Nos. 1, 2, and 4 unbar, replace their handspikes, and resume their posts; takes the breech-sight with the left hand, the roller-handspike with the right, and disposes himself to observe the effect of the shot.

If the elevation is given by a screw, No. 3 turns its handle by direction of the gunner.

No. 3, having passed the hook of the lanyard through the eye of a tube from front to rear, inserts it in the vent, and stretches the lanyard as in No. 107.

At the word, READY, Nos. 1 and 2 take the chocks, and breaking off with the feet farthest from the wall, stand ready to chock the wheels.

7. *Number one* (or the like)—FIRE.

129. Executed as in No. 108.

What is prescribed in No. 109 will apply to this piece.

130. To continue the exercise, the instructor resumes the series of commands, beginning with FROM BATTERY:

To change posts.
To load for action.
To cease firing.
To secure piece, and replace implements.

Executed as in Nos. 111, 112, 113, and 115.

TO LEAVE THE BATTERY.

131. The instructor forms the detachment in rear of the piece, and marches it from the battery as prescribed in No. 12.

132. *Remark*—The service of a gun mounted on a casemate carriage of the old pattern, (which is without the eccentric roller,) will require the following modification: The roller-handspike is dispensed with, and the gunner, at the command, FROM BATTERY, moves two paces to the right.

TO SERVE THE PIECE WITH REDUCED NUMBERS.

Executed as in No. 34.

CHARGES, ETC.

133. The ordinary service charge of powder for heavy guns is *one-fourth* the weight of the shot. For firing double shot it is *one-sixth* that weight.

Range of a 42-pdr., at an elevation of 1° 30′, charge 10½ lbs., - - - - - 860 yards.
Range of a 42-pdr., at an elevation of 5°, charge 10½ lbs., - - - - - 1,055 "
Range of a 32-pdr., at an elevation of 1° 30′, charge 8 lbs., - - - - - 800 "
Range of a 32-pdr., at an elevation of 5°, charge 8 lbs. 1,022 "
Proof range of powder, - - - - 300 "
Greatest elevation the carriage admits, - - 8°
Greatest depression the carriage admits, - - 4°

Wads.
Rapidity of firing.
Penetration of shot.

See Nos. 37, 39, and 40.

8-Inch Columbiad on a Casement Carriage.

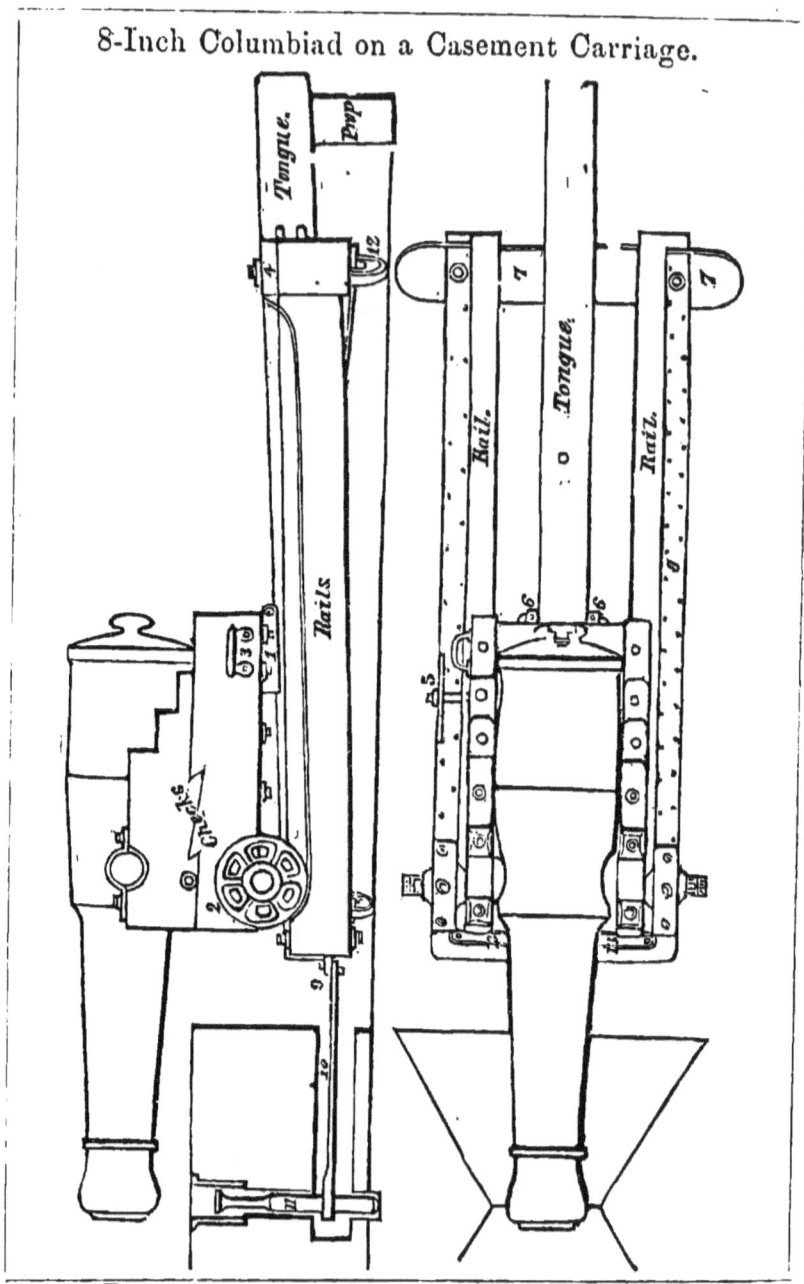

LESSON XIII.

Service of an 8-inch Columbiad mounted on a Casemate Carriage.

Five men are necessary: one gunner and four other cannoneers.
134. The piece is in battery.
 The implements, cct., and their arrangement, are the same as prescribed for the casemate gun in No. 120, substituting *haversack*—worn by No. 4 from the right shoulder to the left side—for *pass-box.*
 The shells are at the magazine, or other safe position, and are brought, as required, to the place prescribed for the budge-barrel.
 135. The instruction for this piece differs in no material respect from that prescribed in Lesson XII.
 It is loaded with shell, which is attached to a sabot. The shell is brought up by No. 4 together with the cartridge, and is set home in the same manner as the ball, except that it is not rammed.

CHARGES, ETC.

136.

Greatest charge of powder,	10 lbs.
Charge of the shell filled with powder,	2 lbs. 9 oz.
Bursting charge of the shell,	1 lb.
Charge to blow out the fuze,	4 oz.
Range at an angle of 1°, ch. 10 lbs. } Axis of the piece 16 ft. }	919 yards.
Range at an angle of 5°, ch. 10 lbs. } above the water. }	1,813 yards.
Proof range of powder,	300 yards.
Weight of shell,	50 lbs.

LESSON XIV.

Service of a 24-pdr. Howitzer mounted on a Flank Casemate Carriage.

Three men are necessary: one gunner and two other cannoneers.
 137. The piece is in battery.

The implements, etc., are arranged as follows:

ROLLER-HANDSPIKE,	Leaning against the scarp wall, behind No. 2.
SPONGE & RAMMER,	Leaning against the scarp wall, behind No. 1, the rammer-head on the ground.
HAVERSACK, - -	Suspended from the knob of the cascable.
TUBE-POUCH, - -	Containing the finger-stall, priming-wire, friction tubes, and the lanyard, wound in St. Andrew's cross upon its handle. Suspended from the knob of the cascable.
VENT-COVER, - -	Covering the vent.
TOMPION, - - -	In the muzzle.
BROOM, - - - -	On the left of the piece.
BUDGE-BARREL, -	Containing cartridges, at the safest and most convenient place in rear of the piece.

The rounds of canister are arranged against the scarp wall, behind No. 2. The shells, if used, are at the magazine, or other safe position, and are brought, as required, to the place prescribed for the budge-barrel.

138. The cannoneers having been marched to their posts, the instructor explains to them the names and uses of the implements, and the nomenclatures of the howitzer, its carriage, and the battery.

139. To cause the implements to be distributed, the instructor commands:

TAKE IMPLEMENTS.

The gunner takes the priming-wire and finger-stall, wearing the latter on the second finger of the right hand; gives the tube-pouch to No. 1, and the haversack to No. 2; takes off the vent-cover and places it against the scarp wall outside of the canisters; seizes the roller-handspike with the right hand, and resumes his post; holding the handspike vertically on the right side, its lower end in line with the toes, the arm extended naturally.

No. 1 equips himself with the tube-pouch.

No. 2 equips himself with the haversack, which he wears from the right shoulder to the left side.

140. The instructor causes the service of the piece to be executed by the following commands:

1. FROM BATTERY.

The gunner, embarring on the left mortise, presses the roller under the rear transom, and seizes the left handle with the left hand.

Nos. 1 and 2 lay hold of the manœuvring rings and handles.

All being ready, the gunner gives the command, HEAVE, and the carriage is run to the rear until the face of the piece is about one yard from the wall, when, disengaging the roller, he commands, HALT. All resume their posts.

2. *Load by Detail*—LOAD.

141. The gunner places himself at the breech; breaks the rear with the right foot; closes the vent with the second finger of the right hand; and manages the elevating screw with the left.

No. 1 seizing the sponge-staff at its middle, brings it across his body; plants the left foot opposite to the muzzle, close to the carriage, and breaks off with the right foot; at the same time throwing the sponge staff into the left hand, back down, and extending both hands towards the ends of the staff, so as to enter the rammer-head into the embrasure and bring the sponge opposite to the muzzle. He then inserts it, and presses it to the bottom of the chamber with three motions.

No. 2 goes for a cartridge, and returns to his post. If shells are used, he brings a shell at the same time.

3. SPONGE.

142. No. 1, using both hands, sponges the chamber carefully; withdraws the sponge, pressing it against the bottom of the bore; turns it over, stepping to his left for this purpose, and rests the rammer-head against the right side of the face of the piece.

No. 2 introduces the cartridge, bottom foremost, seams downward. No. 1 sets it home by three motions, with the right hand.

4. RAM.

143. No. 1, drawing out the rammer to the full extent of his arm, rams once, and throws out the rammer, holding it as before, the rammer-head against the right side of the face of the piece.

No. 2 introduces the canister or shell home with care; throws out the rammer; replaces it; and resumes his post.

The gunner, rising upon the left leg, pricks, leaving the priming-wire in the vent, and resumes his post.

5. IN BATTERY.

144. All apply themselves to the carriage, as prescribed in No. 140, and ease the piece into battery. As soon as it touches the hurters, the gunner commands, HALT. All resume their posts.

6. POINT.

145. No. 1 makes ready a tube, as prescribed for No. 3, in No. 24.

No. 2 goes to the rear of the chassis, and, facing to the front, applies himself to it by hand, in order to traverse it.

The gunner withdraws the priming-wire, and, having pointed the piece, gives the word, READY, making a signal with both hands, at which No. 2 resumes his post; takes out the roller-handspike, and resumes his post.

No. 1 steps to the vent and inserts the tube, holding the lanyard slightly stretched with the right hand, the cord passing between the fingers, back of the hand up, and breaks to his rear a full pace with the left foot, the left hand against the thigh.

7. *Number one* (or the like)—FIRE.

146. No. 1 fires as prescribed for No. 3, in No. 25.

What is prescribed in No. 26 will apply to this piece, substituting No. 1 for No. 3.

147. To continue the exercise, the instructor resumes the series of commands, beginning with FROM BATTERY.

> *To change posts.*
> *To load for action.*
> *To cease firing.*
> *To secure piece, and replace implements.*
> *To leave the battery.*

Executed as in Nos. 111, 112, 113, 114, and 115.

CHARGES, ETC.

148.

Charge of powder,	2 lbs.
Range at an angle of 0°, charge 2 lbs., shell,	295 yards.
Range at an angle of 1°, charge 2 lbs., shell,	516 yards.

Range at an angle of 5°, charge 2 lbs., shell, - - 1,322 yards.
Range at an angle of 2°, charge 1¾ lbs., spher.-case, time 2″, 600 yards.
Range at an angle of 5° 30′, charge 1¾ lbs., spherical-case,
 time 4″, - - - - 1,050 yards.
Range at an angle of 3° 30′, charge 2 lbs., spherical-case,
 time 3″, - - - - 880 yards.
Proof range of powder, - - - 300 yards.
Weight of the 24-pdr. shell, - - - 17 lbs.
Weight of the round of canister, - - 21 lbs.
No. of bullets in a round of canister. - - 48 lbs.

LESSON XV.

Service of an 8-inch Columbiad, mounted on a Columbiad Carriage.

Five men are necessary: one gunner and four other cannoneers.
149. The piece is in battery.
The implements, etc., are arranged as follows:

TRUCK-HAND-SPIKES. { Two on each side of the carriage, laid on the rails, one in rear of each front truck-wheel, and one in rear of each rear truck-wheel.

MANŒUVRING-HANDSPIKES, { One on each side of the carriage, laid on the ground in a line with the cannoneers, opposite to the traverse wheels, the small ends towards the parapet.

ELEVATING-BAR, { Laid across the ties at the junction of the braces, handle to the left.

SPONGE-RAMMER, { One yard behind the cannoneers of the right, the sponge uppermost, the sponge and rammer-heads turned from the parapet, inclined slightly from the piece, and supported upon a prop.

HAVERSACK, - Suspended from the knob of the cascable.

TUBE-POUCH, - { Containing friction tubes, and the lanyard, wound in St. Andrew's cross upon its handle. Suspended from the knob of the cascable.

GUNNER'S-POUCH, { Containing the gunner's level, breech-sight, finger-stall, priming-wire, gunner's gimlet, vent-punch, chalk-line, and chalk. Suspended from the knob of the cascable.

Chocks, - - -	One on each side of the piece, laid on the front of the rails.
Vent-cover, - -	Covering the vent.
Tompion, - - -	In the muzzle.
Broom, - - -	Leaning against the parapet, to the left of the piece.
Budge-barrel, -	Containing cartridges, at the safest and most convenient place in rear of the piece.

When several columbiads are served together, there will be only one gunner's level and two vent-punches to each battery, not exceeding six pieces. To the same battery there will be one *worm* and one *wrench*.

The shells are at the magazine, or other safe position, and are brought, as required, to the place prescribed for the budge-barrel.

150. The cannoneers having been marched to their posts, the instructor explains to them the names and uses of the implements, and the nomenclatures of the columbiad, its carriage, and the battery.

151. To cause the implements to be distributed, the instructor commands:

Take Implements.

The gunner steps to the knob of the cascable; takes off the vent-cover, handing it to No. 2 to place against the parapet, in rear of his post; gives the tube-pouch to No. 3, and the haversack to No. 4; equips himself with his own pouch and the finger-stall, wearing the latter on the second finger of the left hand; takes the elevating bar, and stepping between the rails, levels the piece conveniently for loading; applies his level to verify the line of sight which is marked on the piece, marking it, if necessary, with the chalk line, assisted by No. 2; and resumes his post, holding the elevating-bar with the right hand.

No. 3 equips himself with the tube-pouch.

No. 4 equips himself with the haversack, which he wears from the right shoulder to the left side.

Nos. 1, 2, 3, and 4 take the truck-handspikes with the hand furthest from the parapet, and carry them to that side, holding them vertically, the arm extended naturally.

152. The instructor causes the service of the piece to be executed by the following commands:

1. From Battery.

The gunner moves two paces to the right of his post.

Nos. 1, 2, 3, and 4, facing from the parapet, place the wrenches on the ends of the axle-trees, the handspikes elevated about 30° to the rear, and at the word HEAVE by the gunner, bear down and throw the wheels into gear; Nos. 3 and 4 immediately after laying their handspikes on the platform in front of their posts.

Nos. 1 and 2, facing from the parapet, embar in the most convenient front mortises of the truck-wheels, the hand furthest from the carriage at the top of the handspike, the other hand eight inches lower.

Nos. 3 and 4 go to the assistance of Nos. 1 and 2, and, facing towards them, seize the handspikes with both hands between those of Nos. 1 and 2.

Nos. 1, 2, 3, and 4, in applying themselves to the carriage, to run it from or to battery, break to the rear with the foot nearest to the carriage.

All being ready, the gunner gives the command, HEAVE.

Nos. 1, 2, 3, and 4 act together, and bear upon the handspikes until they are nearly down to the rails, when the gunner commands, UNBAR. Nos. 1 and 2 let go the handspikes with the hand nearest to the carriage, and chock the wheels. Nos. 3 and 4 withdraw the handspikes and pass them to No. 1 and 2, who re-insert them in the front mortises.

The gunner again gives the command, HEAVE, and so on, until the face of the piece is about one yard from the parapet, when he commands, HALT. Nos. 3 and 4 take their posts. Nos. 1 and 2 chock the wheels as before, unbar, and place the wrench of their handspikes on the ends of the axle-tree of the front wheels. At the command OUT OF GEAR by the gunner, they throw the wheels out of gear; lay their handspikes on the rails between the wheels; and take their posts.

2. *Load by Detail*—LOAD.

153. Executed as in Nos. 102 and 103. The gunner, if necessary, adjusts the piece conveniently for loading before closing the vent. No. 4 brings up a shell, together with the cartridge.

3. SPONGE.

154. Executed as in No. 104.

4. Ram.

155. Executed as in No. 105, except that the shell is set carefully home without being rammed.

5. In Battery.

156. Nos. 1 and 2 unchock the wheels, and place the chocks on the ties.

Nos. 1, 2, 3, and 4, facing towards the parapet, apply the wrenches of their handspikes to the ends of the axle-trees; Nos. 1 and 2 so as to throw the front wheels into gear, and Nos. 3 and 4 so as to throw the rear wheels out of gear.

The gunner commands, HEAVE, when the front wheels are thrown into gear.

Should the carriage run too easily after it is in motion, the gunner will command, REAR WHEELS OUT OF GEAR, when the rear wheels are thrown out of gear. Nos. 3 and 4 each take a chock and hold it in front of the rear wheels, ready to apply it under them if necessary.

When the head of the cheeks is about one foot from the end of the rails, the gunner commands, CHOCK, when Nos. 3 and 4 chock the rear wheels. The wheels are unchocked, and the piece is run gently into battery, by Nos. 3 and 4 throwing the rear wheels alternately out of and into gear. As soon as the head of the carriage touches the hurters, the gunner commands, OUT OF GEAR, when the front wheels are thrown out of gear; also the rear wheels, should they be in gear. Nos. 1, 2, 3, and 4 take their posts, and lay their handspikes on the platform just in front of them.

6. Point.

157. No. 3 passes the hook of the lanyard through the eye of a tube from front to rear; holds the handle of the lanyard with the right hand, the hook between the thumb and forefinger; and stands ready to hand it to the gunner.

Nos. 1 and 2, passing outside of the other cannoneers, move to the rear of the chassis, and, each taking one of the manœuvring handspikes, embar with the levelled end under the traverse wheels. For traversing large angles, Nos. 1, 2, 3, and 4 apply themselves by hand at the end of the chassis.

The gunner withdraws the priming-wire; inserts the pawl of the elevating machine in the proper notch by means of the elevating bar, and with the breech-sight gives the required elevation; No. 4 turning the handle of the screw according to his direction.

The moment the piece is correctly pointed, he rises on the left leg, and gives the word READY, making a signal with both hands, at which Nos. 1 and 2 unbar, lay down the handspikes, and resume their post; receives the tube from No. 3, which he inserts in the vent; dismounts from the chassis; and goes to the windward to observe the effect of the shot.

No. 3 stretches the lanyard as in No. 107.

7. *Number one* (or the like)—FIRE.

158. Executed as in No. 108.

What is prescribed in No. 109 will apply to this piece.

159. *Remark.*—If the piece is to be fired at high angles, it is elevated in the following manner:

Nos. 1 and 2—the former carrying his traversing handspike with him—move to the mule; place the handspike in the bore; pass the bight of a trace-rope over it; and bear down slightly on the handspike to enable the gunner to free the pawl from the notch. The gunner draws the pawl back by its handle, and commands EASE AWAY. Nos. 1 and 2, holding the ends of the rope, ease down the breech steadily, until the gunner commands, STEADY, when he inserts the pawl in the proper notch.

160. To continue the exercise, the instructor resumes the series of commands, beginning with FROM BATTERY:

To change posts.
To load for action.
To cease firing.
To secure piece, and replace implements.
To leave the battery.

Executed as in Nos. 111, 112, 113, 114, and 115.

CHAPTER V.

AMMUNITION.

Troops in the field should not only be supplied with a sufficient quantity of ammunition, but the men of the command should be taught how to prepare it. Cartridges for small arms are made of paper, in the following manner: Having prepared the paper, which should be strong, but not too thick, by cutting it first into strips eight and a half inches wide, then cutting these strips crosswise into smaller strips four and a half inches in width, and then cutting these last diagonally, so that the pieces will be three inches on one side and five and a half on the other; the pieces are then rolled on a small cylindrical stick of the same diameter as the ball to be used, about six inches long, having a spherical cavity at one end and rounded at the other. The paper is laid on a table with the side perpendicular to the bases next the workman, the broad end to the left; the stick laid on it with the concave end half an inch from the broad edge of the paper, and enveloped in it once. The right hand is then laid flat on the stick, and all the paper rolled on it. The projecting end of the paper is now neatly folded down into the concavity of the stick, pasted, and pressed on a ball imbedded in the table for the purpose.

Instead of being pasted, these cylinders may be closed by choking with a string, tied to the table, and having at the other end a stick by which to hold it. The convex end of the *former* is placed to the left, and after the paper is rolled on, the *former* is taken in the left hand, and a turn made around it with the choking string half an inch from the end of the paper. Whilst the string is drawn tight with the right hand, the *former* is held in the left with the forefinger resting on the end of the cylinder, folding it neatly down upon the end of the *former*. The choke is then firmly tied with twine.

For ball cartridges, make the cylinders and choke them as above described, and the choke tied without cutting the twine. The *former* is then withdrawn, the ball put in, and the concave end of the

AMMUNITION. 121

former put in after it. The half hitches are made a little above the ball, and the twine cut off.

For ball and buckshot cartridges, make the cylinder as before, insert three buckshot, fasten them with a half hitch, and insert and secure the ball as before.

For buckshot cartridges, make the cylinder as before, insert four tiers of three buckshot each, as at first, making a half hitch between the tiers, and ending with a double hitch.

To fill the cartridges, the cylinders are placed upright in a box, and the charge poured into each from a conical charger of the appropriate size; the mouths of the cylinders are now folded down on the powder by two rectangular folds, and the cartridges bundled in packages of ten. For this a folding box is necessary; it is made with two vertical sides at a distance from each other equal to five diameters of the ball, and two diameters high.

The manner of preparing ammunition for artillery is found in the Manual of Artillery in preceding chapter.

AMMUNITION.

TABLE.
DIMENSIONS OF CARTRIDGE-BAGS.

DIMENSIONS, ETC.	Guns					Columbiads		Howitzers		
	42-pdr.	32-pdr.	24-pdr.	18-pdr.	12-pdr.	10-inch.	8-inch.	8-in. Siege.	10-in. Sea-Coasts.	8-in. Sea-Coasts.
Diameter of cartridge	in. 6.	in. 5.5	in. 5.	in. 4.6	in. 4.2	in. 7.5	in. 6.	in. 4.2	in. 7.5	in. 6.
Length of one pound of powder in a cartridge	.98	1.16	1.45	1.75	2.	.63	.98	2.	.83	.98
Whole length of bag cut	18.	18.	18.	17.	14.	24.	20.	14.	18.	15.
Length of cartridge filled	11.	10.5	9.	7.	6.5	14.	12.5	9.	11.	9.
Usual charge of powder	lbs. 10.5	lbs. 8.	lbs. 6.	lbs. 4.5	lbs. 3.	lbs. 18.	lbs. 10.	lbs. 4.	lbs. 12.	lbs. 8.

Cartridge bags for Siege and Garrison service are usually made of woollen stuff.

INDEX.

FIELD FORTIFICATIONS.

	PAGE.		PAGE.
Abatis,	26	Interior Slope of a Parapet,	5
Attack on Field Works,	40	Inundations,	28
Attacking Houses,	42	Intrenching a Village,	40
" Barricades,	43	Lunette,	12
Banquette,	9	Loopholes,	18, 37
Berme,	9	Lines,	31, 32, 34
Blockhouse,	19	" of Tenailles,	32
Bastioned Lines,	33	" with Intervals or Broken	
Broken Lines,	34	Lines,	34
Barricades,	37	Outlines of Field Works,	10
Caponnière,	14	Octagonal Redoubt,	17
Constructions,	16	" Star Fort,	17
Chevaux-de-frise,	26	Obstacles,	25
Crows Feet,	27	Profile of an Intrenchment,	3
Crémaillère,	32–33	Penetration of Shot,	5
Ditch,	9, 14, 18, 24	Parapet,	5, 8
Double Redans,	14	Plongée,	8
Demi-Bastioned Forts,	18	Pentagonal Redoubt,	16
Defilading of Field Works,	20	Plane of Sight,	20
Distribution of Working Party,	23	" Defilade,	20
Dams,	28, 29	Profiling,	23
Defence of Field Works,	35, 36	Palisades,	25
Exterior Slope of a Parapet,	5	Pointed Stakes,	27
Entanglement,	27	Revetment,	6
Field Works,	3, 40	Redan,	11, 12
Fascines,	6, 7	Redoubt,	12, 16, 17
Fascine Gads,	7	Reduits,	30
Forts with Bastions,	17	Sand Bags,	7
Fraises,	25	Sods of Turf,	8
Fougasses,	27, 28	Superior Slope of the Parapet,	8
Fortifying Houses,	38	Star Fort,	14, 15, 16, 17
Gabions,	6	Stockade Work,	19
Gun Batteries,	8	Thickness of Parapet,	5
Gorges of Works,	27	Terreplein,	9
Hexagonal Redoubt,	17	Triple Redan,	12
" Star Fort,	17	Tambour,	19
Intrenchments, with Flanking		Trous de loup,	26
Arrangements,	4	Têtes de Pont,	30

INDEX.

ARTILLERY, - - - - - 44

	PAGE.		PAGE.
Calibre,	44	Powder,	45
Carcasses,	47	Portfire,	48
Common Case,	48	Ricochet,	45, 49
Canister,	48	Range of Gun,	45
Dispart,	44	Rockets,	47
Guns,	44, 45	Round Shot,	49
Grape Shot,	48	Service Charge of Powder,	45
Gunpowder,	48	Shells,	46, 47
Gun Platform,	49	Shrapnells,	47
Howitzers,	46	Shell Fuze,	48
Hand Grenades,	48	Trunnions,	44
Mortars,	46	Tangent-Scale,	44
Point-Blank,	45, 46	Windage,	44

MANUAL FOR LIGHT ARTILLERY, - 50

Attaching Shafts,	56	Locking Rope,	56
Commands,	52	Moving the Piece by Means of	
Cannoneers,	52	the Cannoneers,	57
Changing Posts,	55	Posts of the Detachments,	51
Coming into Action,	60	Packing,	60, 61, 62
Detachments,	51, 58	Service of the Piece,	52, 55
Duties of the Cannoneers,	52	" several Pieces,	58
Detaching Shafts,	57	Unhitching,	59, 60
Forming the Detachment,	51	Unpacking,	60, 63, 64

MANUAL FOR HEAVY ARTILLERY, - 65

Battery,	66, 70	Service of a 10-inch Siege Mortar	87
Columbiad,	65	Service of an 8-inch Siege Mor-	
Calibre,	66	tar,	93
Casemate,	65	Service of a Coehorn Mortar,	95
Detachments,	66, 67	Service of a 10-inch Sea-Coast	
Flank Casemate,	65	Mortar,	96
Garrison Artillery,	65	Service of a 13-inch Sea-Coast	
Guns,	65	Mortar,	97
Howitzer,	65	Service of a Stone Mortar,	97
Heavy Artillery,	66	Service of a Gun mounted on a	
Implements,	68, 69	Barbette Carriage,	98
Kinds of Ordnance,	66	Service of a Gun mounted on a	
Mortar,	65	Casemate Carriage,	106
Platform,	66	Service of an 8-inch Columbiad	
Service of the Piece,	65	mounted on a Casemate Car-	
Siege Artillery,	65	riage,	111
Sea-Coast Artillery,	65	Service of a 24-pdr. Howitzer	
Service of a Gun mounted on a		mounted on a Flank Casemate	
Siege Carriage,	68	Carriage,	111
Service of an 8-inch Siege How-		Service of an 8 inch Columbiad	
itzer mounted on a 24-pound-		mounted on a Columbiad Car-	
er Siege Carriage,	78	riage,	115

AMMUNITION, - - - - 120

MILITARY BOOKS.

Published and for sale by
J. W. RANDOLPH, RICHMOND, VA.
Also for sale by Booksellers generally.

INSTRUCTIONS

For Officers and Non-Commissioned Officers of Cavalry, on Outpost Duty.

BY

LIEUT. COL. VON ARENTSCHILDT,

First Hussars King's German Legion:

With an Abridgement of them by

LIEUT. COL., THE HON. F. PONSONBY,
Twelfth Light Dragoons.   Price—50 Cents.

DIRECTIONS
FOR
COOKING BY TROOPS
IN
CAMP AND HOSPITAL.

Prepared for the Army. With Essays on
"TAKING FOOD" AND "WHAT FOOD."
BY
FLORENCE NIGHTINGALE.

Price—25 Cents.

THE HAND BOOK
OF
ARTILLERY.
BY
CAPTAIN JOSEPH ROBERTS,

Price—75 Cents.   Fourth Regiment Artillery. U. S. Army.

SKIRMISH DRILL
FOR
MOUNTED TROOPS.
By Capt. D. H. MAURY, C. S. A.

COOPER'S
CAVALRY TACTICS
AND A
MANUAL FOR COLT'S REVOLVER.

Price—65 Cents.   With Plates.

Capt. VIELE'S
HAND BOOK
OF
FIELD FORTIFICATIONS AND ARTILLERY;
ALSO A
MANUAL FOR LIGHT AND HEAVY ARTILLERY,

Price—$1 25.   With Plates.

SCIENCE OF WAR!
TACTICS
FOR
OFFICERS
OF
INFANTRY, CAVALRY AND ARTILLERY.

Arranged and Compiled by
L. v. BUCKHOLTZ.
One Volume, 12mo. Price—75 Cents.

INFANTRY CAMP DUTY, FIELD FORTIFICATION, AND COAST DEFENSE.

Prepared and Arranged by
Capt. L. v. BUCKHOLTZ.
With Plates. 16mo., muslin. Price—50 Cents.

Will be Published October 10th, 1861;

HAND BOOK
FOR
ACTIVE SERVICE.
CONTAINING

Practical Instructions in Campaign Duties—The Recruit—The Company—The Regiment—The March—The Camp—Guard and Guard-Mounting—Rations, and Mode of Cooking Them. With Illustrations.

By EGBERT L. VIELE,
LATE U. S. A.

Captain Engineers, Seventh Regiment, N. G.

Price— 75 Cents.

"If this be Treason, make the most of it."

ANTICIPATIONS OF THE FUTURE,
TO SERVE AS
LESSONS FOR THE PRESENT TIME.

In the form of EXTRACTS OF LETTERS from an English Resident in the United States, to the London Times, from 1864 to 1870.

With an APPENDIX on the Causes and Consequences of the Independence of the South.

By EDMUND RUFFIN.

12mo. muslin, 426 pages. Price $1; or $1 25 by mail.

PLANTATION BOOK.
PLANTATION AND FARM INSTRUCTION,
REGULATION, RECORD,
INVENTORY AND ACCOUNT BOOK.

For the use of Managers of Estates, and for the better ordering and management of plantation and farm business in many particulars.

BY A SOUTHERN PLANTER.

"Order is Heaven's first law."

New and improved edition, cap folio, half calf; price $1 50. Also a larger edition, for COTTON PLANTATIONS. price $2. Either sent by mail, post paid, for 25 cents extra.

SOUTHERN BOOK PUBLISHING HOUSE,

ESTABLISHED 1833.

J. W. RANDOLPH,

BOOKSELLER, PUBLISHER, STATIONER

AND

MUSIC DEALER,

Offers on the best terms for cash or approved credit, the largest *assortment* of goods in his line to be found south of Philadelphia.

THE STOCK EMBRACES

LAW, MEDICINE, THEOLOGY,
    HISTORY, BIOGRAPHY, POLITICS,
        SCHOOL, CLASSICS, JUVENILE, NOVELS,
            POETRY, and MISCELLANEOUS BOOKS,

In English and other languages.

Particular attention given to the collection of Rare Works. Books imported to order.

AMERICAN,
    ENGLISH
        AND
            FRENCH STATIONERY,

Of the best quality.

A large stock of STANDARD MUSIC, and all the New Popular Pieces are for sale soon as published.

BLANK BOOKS made to order, and all kinds of **BOOK-BINDING** executed in good style.

CATALOGUES will be mailed to all who send five cents to pay the postage.

OLD BOOKS

Taken in Exchange for New Works.

J. W. RANDOLPH,
121 MAIN STREET, RICHMOND, VA.

BOOKS!
OFFERED TO THE TRADE AND FOR SALE BY
J. W. RANDOLPH,
121 Main street, Richmond, Va.

LAW.

HALL'S (EVERARD) DIGESTED INDEX OF THE VIRGINIA REPORTS, containing all the points argued and determined in the Court of Appeals of Virginia, from Washington to third Leigh, inclusive, with a table of the names of cases reported, 2 vols. 8vo, sheep, Richmond, 1825 and '35... $3 00

HENING & MUNFORD. REPORTS OF CASES argued and determined in the Supreme Court of Appeals of Virginia, with select cases relating chiefly to points of practice decided by the Superior Court of Chancery for the Richmond District, by W. W. Hening and W. Munford, a new and *only complete* edition, with memoirs of the Judges whose decisions are reported; the present rules of the Court of Appeals, and of the Chancery Court in Richmond; references to subsequent decisions of the Court of Appeals, and to existing statutes in *paria materia*, with the points herein reported, and a list of the cases overruled. Edited by B. B. Minor, L. B., 4 vols. 8vo, sheep, Richmond, 1854.............. 20 00

JEFFERSON'S (THOMAS) REPORTS OF CASES determined in the General Court of Virginia from 1730 to 1740, and from 1768 to 1772, half calf, Charlottesville, 1829, 2 50

LAWYER'S GUIDE. THE AMERICAN PLEADER AND LAWYER'S GUIDE, in commencing, prosecuting and defending actions at common law and suits in equity, with full and correct precedents of pleadings in the several cases which most frequently occur, adapted to the practice of the United States, by W. W. Hening, 2 vols. 8vo, sheep, New York, 1811 and '26............................ 8 00

MATTHEW'S (J. M.) GUIDE TO COMMISSIONERS IN CHANCERY, with practical Forms for the discharge of their duties, adapted to the new Code of Virginia, 8vo, sheep, Richmond, 1850............................ 2 50

MATTHEW'S DIGEST OF THE LAWS OF VIRGINIA, of a civil nature and of a permanent character, and a general operation, illustrated by judicial decisions, to which are

prefixed the Constitutions of the United States and Virginia, by J. M. Matthews, 2 vols. 8vo, sheep, Richmond, 1856-7, ... 12 00
THE SAME INTERLEAVED WITH WRITING PAPER FOR NOTES, 2 vols. ... 17 00
MUNFORD'S (WILLIAM) REPORTS OF CASES argued and determined in the Supreme Court of Appeals of Virginia, 6 vols. 8vo, sheep, Richmond and New York, 1812, &c. ... 36 00
PATTON & HEATH. A GENERAL INDEX TO GRATTAN'S REPORTS, from second to eleventh, inclusive, by J. M. Patton and R. B. Heath, 8vo, sheep, Richmond, 1856. ... 3 50
PATTON & HEATH. REPORTS OF CASES decided in the Special Court of Appeals of Virginia, held at Richmond, and a General Index to Grattan's Reports, from 2d to 11th vol., inclusive, by J. M. Patton and R. B. Heath, vol. 1, 8vo, sheep, Richmond, 1856. ... 6 00
PATTON & HEATH. REPORTS OF CASES decided in the Special Court of Appeals, held in Richmond 1855-6-7, by J. M. Patton and R. B. Heath, 2 vols. 8vo, sheep, Richmond, 1855-7. ... 7 00
QUARTERLY LAW JOURNAL, A. B. Guigon, Editor, vol. 1, 1856, vol. 2, 1857, vol. 3, 1858, vol. 4, 1859, 8vo, sheep, Richmond, per volume. ... 5 00
RANDOLPH'S (PEYTON) REPORTS OF CASES argued and determined in the Court of Appeals of Virginia, 6 vols. 8vo, sp. Richmond, Va., 1823, &c. ... 24 00
RITCHIE'S (THOMAS, Jr.) TRIAL. A full report, embracing all the evidence and arguments in the case of the Commonwealth of Virginia vs. T. Ritchie, Jr., for the killing of John Hampden Pleasants, to which is added an appendix showing the action of the Court in relation to the other parties connected with the said case, 8vo, paper, New York, 1846. ... 25
VIRGINIA. PAY AND MUSTER ROLLS OF THE VIRGINIA MILITIA IN THE WAR OF 1812, 8vo half calf, Richmond, 1851-2. ... 15 00
VIRGINIA CASES. A Collection of Cases decided by the General Court of Virginia, chiefly relating to the Penal Laws of the Commonwealth, commencing 1789 and ending 1826, copied from the Records of the said Court, with explanatory notes, by Judges Brockenbrough and Holmes, second edition, with abstracts prefixed to the cases, 2 vols. in 1, 8vo, sheep, Richmond, 1826 and 1853 ... 6 00
VIRGINIA LAW OF CORPORATIONS, ACTS OF THE GENERAL ASSEMBLY compiled from the code of Virginia, together with an act passed in 1837, relating to Manufacturing and Mining Companies, 8vo, paper, Richmond, 1853. ... 50

WYTHE'S (GEO.) REPORTS. Decisions of cases in Virginia of the High Court of Chancery, with remarks upon Decrees by the Court of Appeals, reversing some of those decisions, by George Wythe, 2d and only complete edition. With a Memoir of the author, Analysis of the Cases, and an Index, by B. B. Minor, L. B. And with an Appendix, containing references to cases in *pari materia*, an essay on lapse, joint tenants and tenants in common, &c., &c., by Wm. Green, Esq. 8vo, sheep. Richmond, 1852........ 4 00
WHITE ACRE *vs.* BLACK ACRE, a Case at Law, reported by J. G., Esq., a retired barrister of Lincolnshire, England, 18mo, mus., Richmond, 1856................. 75
VIRGINIA. RULES OF THE COURT OF APPEALS from its establishment to the present time. Also, Rules of the District Courts of Fredericksburg and Williamsburg. 8vo., paper. Richmond.. 10
GILMER'S (F. W.) VIRGINIA REPORTS. 8vo., calf. Richmond, 1821... 2 00
GRATTAN'S (P. R.) VIRGINIA REPORTS. 15 vols., 8vo, calf. Richmond, 1845-60. Per volume........... 4 00
LEIGH'S (B. W.) VIRGINIA REPORTS. 12 vols., 8vo, calf. Richmond, 1830-44. Per volume................ 4 00
ROBINSON'S (C.) VIRGINIA REPORTS. 2 vols., 8vo, calf. Richmond, 1843-4. Per volume................. 4 00
HENING (W. W.) & SHEPHERD'S (S.) STATUTES OF VIRGINIA from 1619 to 1807. 16 vols., 8vo, sheep. Richmond, 1823-36.. 13 00
VIRGINIA ACTS OF ASSEMBLY from 1808 to 1860. 8vo, half sheep. Richmond ....
SELECTIONS OF THE MOST IMPORTANT PORTIONS OF THE REPORTS OF THE REVISOR'S OF VIRGINIA CODE. With notes by A. H. Sands. 8vo, sheep. In press..

POLITICS.

TUCKER'S (H. ST. GEORGE) LECTURES ON NATURAL LAW, also Lectures on Government, 12mo, muslin, Charlottesville, 1844....................................... 75
ANTICIPATIONS OF THE FUTURE, TO SERVE AS LESSONS FOR THE PRESENT TIME. Extracts from letters written from Washington to the London Times during the years 1864-5-6-7-8. 12mo, mus., Richmond, 1860.. 1 00
TUCKER'S (H. ST. GEORGE) LECTURES ON CONSTITUTIONAL LAW, for the use of the Law Class of the University of Virginia, 12mo, mus., Richmond, 1843.. 75
VIRGINIA POLITICS. A History of the Political Campaign in Va. in 1855, to which is added a review of the position of parties in the Union, and a statement of the political issues distinguishing them on the eve of the Presi-

dential Campaign of 1856, by J. P. Hambleton, M. D., 8vo, mus., Richmond, 1856..... .... 2 50
VIRGINIA CONVENTION. Proceeding and Debates of the Va. State Convention of 1829-30, to which are subjoined the new Constitution of Virginia, and the votes of the people, 8vo, calf, Richmond, 1830.................. 5 00
VIRGINIA STATISTICS. Documents containing statistics ordered to be printed by the State Convention sitting in the city of Richmond, 1850-51, 8vo, calf, Richmond, 1851.. 2 50
VIRGINIA CONVENTION. Journal, Acts and Proceedings of a General Convention of the State of Virginia assembled at Richmond 1850, 8vo, half calf, Richmond, 1850. 5 00
VIRGINIA CONVENTION 1850-51. Register of the Debates and Proceedings of the Virginia Reform Convention, (imperfect,) 8vo, half sheep, Richmond, 1851........... 3 00
VIRGINIA. Journal of the Senate and House of Delegates for various years. Richmond.
VIRGINIA. Journal of the Convention of 1776. 4to, half sheep. Richmond, 1816......................... 2 00
ELLETT'S ESSAYS ON THE LAW OF TRADE, in reference to the Works of Internal Improvement in the U. S. 8vo, mus., Richmond, 1839.. .... 1 50
LETTERS OF CURTIUS, written by the late John Thomson, of Petersburg; to which is added a Speech delivered by him in August, '95, on the British Treaty; to which a short Sketch of his Life is prefixed. 12mo, paper. Richmond, 1804.. .... 1 00
JEFFERSON. Memoir, Correspondence and Miscellanies from the Papers of Thomas Jefferson. Edited by Thomas Jefferson Randolph. 4 vols., 8vo, boards. Charlottesville, 1829....... .... 5 00
JEFFERSON. Observations on the Writings of Thomas Jefferson, with particular reference to the attack they contain on the Memory of the late Gen'l Henry Lee. In series of letters, by H. Lee. 2nd edition. With an Introduction and Notes, by Charles C. Lee. 8vo, mus. Philadelphia, 1839............................. 1 75
LONDON (D. H.) ON THE COMMERCIAL, AGRICULTURAL AND INTELLECTUAL INDEPENDENCE OF VIRGINIA AND THE SOUTH. 8vo, paper. Richmond, 1860..................................... 25
VIRGINIAN (THE) HISTORY OF THE AFRICAN COLONIZATION. (This contains, among other documents, portions of the Debate on Slavery in the Virginia Legislature of 1832.) Edited by Rev. P. Slaughter. 8vo, mus., Richmond, 1855.. .... 1 00
RUFFIN'S (EDMUND) AFRICAN COLONIZATION UNVEILED. Slavery and Free Labor described and

compared. The Political Economy of Slavery; or, the Institution considered in regard to its influence on public wealth and the general welfare. Two Great Evils of Virginia, and their one Common Remedy, 8vo, pa. Richmond, 1860. The four pamphlets, each.................. 10

HISTORY.

BEVERLY'S (ROBERT) HISTORY OF VIRGINIA. In four parts. I. The history of the settlement of Virginia, and the government thereof, to the year 1706. II. The natural productions and conveniences of the country, suited to trade and improvement. III. The native Indians, their religion, laws and customs, in war and peace. IV. The present state of the country, as to the polity of the government, and the improvements of the land, to 10th of June, 1720. By Robert Beverly, a native of the place. Re-printed from the author's second revised London edition of 1792, with an introduction by Charles Campbell, author of the "Colonial History of Virginia." 14 plates, 8vo, mus. Richmond, 1855......................... 2 50

AN ACCOUNT OF DISCOVERIES IN THE WEST until 1519, and of Voyages to and along the Atlantic Coast of North America from 1520 to 1573. Prepared for the Virginia Historical and Philosophical Society, by Conway Robinson. 8vo, mus. Richmond, 1848. (Published at $5.) 2 50

JEFFERSON'S (THOMAS) NOTES ON THE STATE OF VIRGINIA. A new edition, prepared by the author, containing many new notes never before published.

It is printed from President Jefferson's copy (Stockdale's London edition of 1787) of the Notes on Virginia, with his last additions (they are numerous) and corrections in manuscript, and four maps of Caves, Mounds, Fortifications, &c.

Letters from Gen. Dearborn and Judge Gibson, relating to the Murder of Logan, &c.

Fry and Jefferson's Map of Virginia, Maryland, Delaware, and Pennsylvania—very valuable on account of the Public Places and Private Residences, which are not to be found on any other Map.

A Topographical Analysis of Virginia, for 1790—a curious and useful sheet for historical reference.

Translations of all Jefferson's Notes in Foreign Languages, by Prof. Schele de Vere, of the University of Virginia.

8vo, mus. Richmond, 1853......................... 2 50

SMITH'S (M.) GEOGRAPHICAL VIEW OF THE BRITISH POSSESSIONS IN NORTH AMERICA. 18mo, sheep. Baltimore, 1814........................ 35

VIRGINIA CONVENTION OF 1776: Historical and Biographical. By H. B. Grigsby. 8vo, mus. Richmond, 1855. 1 50
OREGON, OUR RIGHT AND TITLE: containing an account of the condition of the Oregon Territory, its soil, climate and geographical position; together with a statement of the claims of Russia, Spain, Great Britain, and the United States. Accompanied with a map prepared by the author. By Wyndham Robertson, jr., of Virginia. 8vo, paper. Washington, 1846.. 50
HOT SPRINGS. The Invalid's Guide to the Virginia Hot Springs, with cases illustrative of their effects. By Thos. Goode, M. D. 32mo, cloth. Richmond, 1846.......... 25
VIRGINIA. Report on the Soils of Powhatan County. By W. Gilham, Prof. Va. Military Institute. With a Map. 8vo, paper Richmond, 1857......'................... 35
BIRD. WESTOVER MANUSCRIPTS, containing the history of the dividing line betwixt Virginia and North Carolina. A Journey to the Land of Eden, A. D. 1733; and A Progress to the Mines, written from 1728-36, and now first published. By W. Bird, of Westover. 8vo, boards. Petersburg, 1841. New edition in press................ 3 00
BLAND PAPERS, being a selection from the manuscripts of Col. T. Bland, jr., of Prince George county, Va.; to which are prefixed an Introduction and Memoir edited by Charles Campbell. 2 vols. in one, 8vo, h'f ro. Petersburg, 1840.. .... 3 00
VIRGINIA POLITICS. A History of the Political Campaign in Virginia in 1855; to which is added a review of the position of Parties in the Union, and a statement of the political issues distinguishing them on the eve of the Presidential Campaign of 1856. By J. P. Hambleton, M. D. 8vo, mus. Richmond, 1856...................... 2 50
VIRGINIA CONVENTION. Proceeding and Debates of the Virginia State Convention of 1829-30, to which are subjoined the New Constitution of Virginia, and the votes of the people. 8vo, calf. Richmond, 1830............. 5 00
VIRGINIA. Pay and Muster Rolls of the Virginia Militia in the War of 1812. 8vo, half calf. Richmond, 1851-2. 15 00
VIRGINIA STATISTICS. Documents constaining statistics ordered to be printed by the State Convention sitting in the city of Richmond, 1850-51. 8vo, calf. Richmond, 1851... 2 50
VIRGINIA CONVENTION. Journal, Acts and Proceedings of a General Convention of the State of Virginia, assembled at Richmond, 1850. 8vo, half calf. Richmond, 1850... 5 00
VIRGINIA HISTORICAL SOCIETY COLLECTIONS, ADDRESSES, &c. (Contents: Stuart's Indian Wars, 1763; Grace Sherwood's Trial, 1705; Address in 1833 by

J. P. Cushing; in 1851 by W. H. Macfarland; in 1852 by H. A. Washington; in 1853 by H. B. Grigsby; in 1856 by R. M. T. Hunter; in 1856 by J P. Holcombe.) 8vo, half turkey. Richmond, 1833-56....... .... 5 00

VIRGINIA CONVENTION, 1850-51. Register of the Debates and Proceedings of the Virginia Reform Convention, (imperfect.) 8vo, half sheep. Richmond, 1851........ 3 00

VIRGINIA. A Comprehensive Description of Virginia and the District of Columbia, containing a copious collection of geographical, statistical, political, commercial, religious, moral and miscellaneous information, chiefly from original sources, by Joseph Martin; to which is added a History of Virginia, from its first settlement to the year 1754, with an abstract of the principal events from that period to the Independence of Virginia, by W. H. Brockenbrough, formerly Librarian at the University of Virginia, and afterwards Judge of the United States Court of Florida, 8vo, sp. Richmond........................ 2 00

MAURY. Paper on the Gulf Stream and Currents of the Sea, read before the National Institute at its annual meeting in 1844, by M. F. Maury, Lieut. U. S. Navy. 8vo, pa. Richmond, 1844........ 13

BURKE. The Virginia Mineral Springs, with remarks on their use, the Diseases to which they are applicable, and in which they are contra-indicated; accompanied by a Map of Routes and Distances. A new work—2d edition. Improved and enlarged. By W. Burke, M. D. 12mo, muslin. Richmond, 1853........................... 75

COTTOM'S EDITION OF RICHARDSON'S ALMANAC. 24mo, paper, 6c. Per dozen, 25c; per gross, $2.50. Containing, besides the twelve calendar pages and astronomical calculations, a Jewish Calendar, Gardener's Monthly Instructor, List of the Virginia Senators, Members of Congress, Senate and House of Delegates; Virginia and North Carolina State Governments; State and Federal Courts of Virginia, North Carolina, Maryland, and the District of Columbia; Conjectures of the Weather, Equation or Time Tables, Receipts, Anecdotes, &c. Published annually.

JEFFERSON & CABELL. Early history of the University of Virginia, as contained in the Letters of (during the years from 1810 to 1826) Thos. Jefferson and Joseph C. Cabell, hitherto unpublished; with an Appendix consisting of Mr. Jefferson's bill for a complete system of education, and other illustrative documents; and an Introduction, comprising a brief historical sketch of the University, and a biographical notice of Joseph C. Cabell. 8vo, muslin. Richmond, 1856...................... 2 50

JUBILEE AT JAMESTOWN, VA. Report of Proceedings in Commemoration of the 13th of May, the Second

Centesimal Anniversary of the Settlement of Virginia,
containing the Order of Procession, the Prayer of Bishop
Madison, the Orations, the Odes and Toasts; together
with the Proceedings at Williamsburg on the 15th, the
day when the Convention of Virginia assembled in the old
Capitol, declared her Independent, and recommended a
similar procedure to Congress, and to the other States.
8vo, paper. Petersburg, 1807........................ 1 00
VIRGINIA. Journal of the Senate and House of Delegates
for various years. Richmond.
VIRGINIA. Journal of the Convention of 1776. 4to, half
sheep. Richmond, 1816...... .... 2 00
JEFFERSON. Memoir, Correspondence and Miscellanies
from the Papers of Thos. Jefferson. Edited by Thos.
Jefferson Randolph. 4 vols., 8v, boards. Charlottesville,
1829.. .... 5 00
JEFFERSON. Observations on the Writings of Thomas
Jefferson, with particular reference to the attack they
contain on the Memory of the late Gen'l Henry Lee. In
* series of letters by H. Lee. 2nd edition. With an Introduction and Notes, by Chas. C. Lee. 8vo, mus. Philadelphia, 1839. .... 1 75

AGRICULTURE.

RUFFIN'S (EDMUND) FARMER'S REGISTER. 10
vols., 8vo, half roan................................ 30 00
RUFFIN'S (EDMUND) PRIZE ESSAY ON AGRICULTURAL EDUCATION. 2nd edition, 8vo, paper....... 10
RUFFIN'S (EDMUND) AGRICULTURAL ESSAYS:
Containing articles on the theory and practice of draining
(in all its branches:) advantages of ploughing flat land
in wide beds; on clover culture and the use and value of
the products; management of wheat harvests; harvesting
corn fodder; on the manner of propagation and habits of
the moth or weevil, and means to prevent its ravages;
inquiry into the causes of the existence of prairies, savannas and deserts, and the peculiar condition of soils which
favor or prevent the growth of trees; depressed condition
of lower Virginia; apology for "book farmers;" fallow;
usefulness of snakes; embanked tide marshes and mill
ponds as causes of disease; on the sources of malaria, or
of autumnal diseases, and means of prevention; on the
culture, uses and value of the southern pea, (Ruffin's Prize
Essay of November, 1854,) and especially as a manuring
crop. 12mo, half bound. Richmond, 1855............ 1 25
RUFFIN. An Essay on Calcareous Manures. By Edmund
Ruffin, a practical farmer of Virginia from 1812; founder
and sole editor of the Farmer's Register; Member and

Secretary of the former State Board of Agriculture; formerly Agricultural Surveyor of the State of South Carolina; and President of the Virginia State Agricultural Society. 5th edition, amended and enlarged, with plates. Fine edition, 8vo, library style, $2; cheap edition, 12mo, half roan or mus. Richmond, 1852.................... 1 25

PLANTATION AND FARM INSTRUCTION, Regulation, Record, Inventory, and Account Book, and for the better Ordering and Management of Plantation and Farm Business in every particular. By a Southern Planter. "Order is Heaven's First Law." *New edition printing.*

THEOLOGY.

MAGRUDER & ORVIS' DEBATE on the Punishment of the Wicked, and on the Kingdom of God. 12mo, muslin. Richmond, 1855.. 75

WALSH'S (REV. J. T.) NATURE AND DURATION OF FUTURE PUNISHMENT. 12mo, muslin. Richmond, 1857... 50

MEMOIR AND SERMONS OF THE REV. WILLIAM DUVALL, City Missionary. By the Rev. C. Walker. With a portrait. 12mo, mus. Richmond, 1854......... 50

STRINGFELLOW'S (T., D.D.) STATISTICAL AND SCRIPTURAL VIEW OF SLAVERY. 4th edition, 12mo, mus. Richmond, 1856......................... 50

FAMILY CHRISTIAN ALBUM. Edited by Mrs. E P. Elam. 8vo, mus. Richmond, 1855.................... 1 50

FLAVEL'S WORKS. Balm of the Covenant. View of the Soul of Man, &c. 8vo, half roan. Richmond, 1828.. 60

BLAIR. Sermons of Rev. John D. Blair, collected from his manuscripts. 8vo, sheep. Richmond, 1825............ 50

POETRY.

BARTLEY'S (J. AVIS) POEMS. Lays of Ancient Virginia, &c. 12mo, mus. Richmond, 1855............... 75

MOCK (THE) AUCTION. Ossawatamie Sold! A Mock Heroic Poem; with Portraits and Tableaux, illustrative of the character and actions of the world-renowned Order of Peter Funks. By a Virginian. 12mo, mus. 10 tinted plates. Richmond, 1860............................ 75

CARTER. Mugæ, by Nugator; or Pieces in Prose and Verse. By St. Ledger L. Carter. 24mo, half roan. Baltimore, 1844...................................... 75

BETHEL HYMNS. A Collection of Original Spiritual Songs. By Mrs Elizabeth Sowers, of Clark county, Va. 48mo, sheep. Richmond, 1849...................... 25

FARMER'S (C. M.) FAIRY OF THE STREAM, and other Poems. 12mo, boards. Richmond, 1847.......... 50

COURTNEY'S (REV J.) SELECTION OF HYMNS. 24mo, sheep. Richmond, 1831..................... 35

SCHOOL.

VAUGHAN'S (S. A.) ABECEDARIAN; OR, FIRST BOOK FOR CHILDREN. Designed to render the learning of the Alphabet, and of Elementary Spelling and Defining, pleasing and intellectual; and to fix in the mind habits of attention to the force of letters in the formation of words, and to the meaning of words, and through their application to their appropriate objects, to inculcate the love of Nature and reverence of Nature's God. 12mo, roan back. Richmond....................................... 15
YOUNG (THE) AMERICAN'S PRIMER, OR FIRST BOOK. 24mo, paper. Richmond, per dozen.......... 25
SCHOOLER'S (SAMUEL) ELEMENTS OF DESCRIPTIVE GEOMETRY, the Point, the Straight Line, and the Plane. 4to, mus. Richmond, 1853............... 2 00
    The paper, type, and plates, are in the finest style of the arts; and the book, altogether, has been pronounced equal, if not superior, to any English, French, or American work on the subject.
GARNETT'S (JAMES M.) LECTURES ON FEMALE EDUCATION, AND THE GOSSIP'S MANUAL. 3rd edition, 18mo, sheep. Richmond, 1825.......... 50
CÆSAR, with English Notes. By Samuel Schooler. *In preparation.*

SLAVERY.

STRINGFELLOW'S (T., D.D.) STATISTICAL AND SCRIPTURAL VIEW OF SLAVERY. Fourth edition, 12mo, mus. Richmond, 1856........................ 50
FLETCHER'S (JOHN) STUDIES ON SLAVERY. 8vo, sheep. Natchez, 1852................................. 2 00
DEW. An Essay on Slavery. By T. R. Dew, late President of William and Mary College. 2d edition, 8vo, paper. Richmond, 1849.. 50
RUFFIN'S (EDMUND) AFRICAN COLONIZATION UNVEILED. Slavery and Free Labor described and compared. The political Economy of Slavery; or the Institution considered in regard to its influence on public wealth and the general welfare. Two Great Evils of Virginia, and their one Common Remedy. 8vo, pa. Richmond, 1860. Each.. 10
UNCLE ROBIN IN HIS CABIN IN VIRGINIA, AND TOM WITHOUT ONE IN BOSTON. By J. W. Page. 2nd edition, plates, 12mo, muslin. Richmond, 1853..... 75
WHITE ACRE *vs.* BLACK ACRE, a Case at Law, reported by J. G., Esq., a retired barrister of Lincolnshire, England, 18mo, mus. Richmond, 1856................. 75

MASONIC.

DOVE'S (JOHN) VIRGINIA TEXT BOOK OF ROYAL ARCH MASONRY. Plates, 12mo, mus. Richmond, 1853,	1 25
DOVE'S (JOHN) HISTORY OF THE GRAND LODGE OF VIRGINIA, AND ANCIENT CONSTITUTIONS OF MASONRY. 18mo, muslin. Richmond, 1854.....	75
DOVE'S (JOHN, M.D.) MASONIC TEXT BOOK. 2nd edition. Plates, 12mo, mus. Richmond, 1854..........	1 25

NOVELS.

REMINISCENCES OF A VIRGINIA PHYSICIAN. By Prof. P. S. Ruter. 2 vols., 12mo, paper. Louisville, 1849,	50
SOUTHERN AND SOUTH-WESTERN SKETCHES. Fun, Sentiment and Adventure! Edited by a Gentleman of Richmond. 18mo, mus. Richmond...............	60
TUCKER. Gertrude. A Novel. By Judge Tucker, Professor of William and Mary College. 8vo, paper. Richmond, 1845..	35
UNCLE ROBIN IN HIS CABIN IN VIRGINIA. AND TOM WITHOUT ONE IN BOSTON. By J. W. Page. 2nd edition, plates, 12mo, mus. Richmond, 1853........	75
SKETCHES OF CHARACTER, (Randolph, Wirt, Kenton, &c.) AND TALES FOUNDED ON FACT. By F. W. Thomas. 8vo, boards. Louisville, 1849........	25
MICHAEL BONHAM, OR THE FALL OF BEXAR. A Tale of Texas. In five parts. By a Southerner. 8vo, paper. Richmond, 1852............................	25
EDITH ALLEN, OR SKETCHES OF LIFE IN VIRGINIA. By Lawrence Neville. 12mo, mus. Richmond, 1855..	1 00

MUSIC.

EVERETT'S (Dr. A. B.) ELEMENTS OF VOCAL MUSIC; including a Treatise on Harmony, and a Chapter on Versification. Designed as a text-book for teachers and pupils in Female Seminaries, Male Academies, Singing Classes, etc., etc., and for private study and reference. 2nd and enlarged edition. 18mo, mus. Richmond, 1860,	50
EVERETT'S (L. C. & Dr. A. B.) NEW THESAURUS MUSICUS, OR U. S. COLLECTION OF CHURCH MUSIC; constituting the most complete variety of new Psalm and Hymn Tunes, Sentences, Anthems, Chants, &c. for the use of the Choir, the Congregation and the Singing School, ever offered to the American people. Comprising also all the popular old choir and congregational tunes in general use. Music, 8vo, boards. Richmond, 1860.....:...	1 00

WINKLER'S HINTS TO PIANO-FORTE PLAYERS. 12mo, boards. Richmond, 1847...................... 25

MISCELLANY.

LUMBER (THE) DEALER'S ASSISTANT, OR COMPLETE TABLES OF THE MEASUREMENTS OF TIMBER, &c.—showing the quantity in feet and inches in any number of plank or scantling, from one to fifty; of any length in feet or half feet, from eight to twenty-two feet long; of any width in inches and half inches, from three to twenty inches wide. By George S. Sutherlin. 12mo, half sheep. Richmond, 1849................... 50
VIRGINIA JUSTICE'S RECORD BOOK OF JUDGMENTS. Cap size, half bound...................... 1 50
PAJOT'S OBSTETRIC TABLES, translated from the French, and arranged by O. A. Grenshaw, M. D., and J. B. McCaw, M. D. 4to, boards. Richmond, 1856....... 1 25
PHYSICIAN'S TABULATED DIARY, designed to facilitate the study of Disease at the Bedside. By a Physician of Virginia. Pocket size. Muslin. Richmond, 1856.... 50
SOUTHERN LITERARY MESSENGER. 29 vols., 8vo, in numbers. Richmond, 1834-59.....................100 00
☞ Most of the volumes or numbers are for sale separate.
RANDOLPH'S POCKET DIARY AND DAILY MEMODANDUM BOOK. Richmond, 186—. 18mo, half bound, 35c.; tucks.. 60
RANDOLPH'S POCKET DIARY, DAILY MEMORANDUM AND ACCOUNT BOOK. Richmond, 186—. Half bound, 75c.; tucks.................................... 1 00
LIBRARY CASES, OR BOXES, in neat book form, very convenient and useful for preserving valuable pamphlets and magazines. 8vo. roan back...................... 60
SKETCHES OF CHARACTER, (Randolph, Wirt, Kenton, &c.,) AND TALES FOUNDED ON FACT. By F. W. Thomas. 8vo, boards. Louisville, 1849......... 25
EDGAR'S SPORTSMAN'S HERALD & STUD BOOK 8vo, sp. New York, 1833....... .... 1 50
WATER CURE. By Dr. J. B. Williams, and others. With comments and explanatory remarks on bathing for invalids, &c., by J. Timberlake. 18mo, paper. Richmond, 1853.. 25
THE PRACTICAL MINER'S OWN BOOK & GUIDE. By J. Budge. With additions by J. Atkins. Plates, 12mo, muslin. Richmond, 1860............................. 2 00
THE CARPENTER'S GUIDE IN STAIR-BUILDING AND HAND-RAILING, based upon Plain and Practical Principles, with sufficient explanations to inform without confusing the learner. By Patrick O'Neill, Practical Stair-Builder. Folio, mus. Richmond................. 2 00

www.ingramcontent.com/pod-product-compliance
Lightning Source LLC
Chambersburg PA
CBHW030339170426
43202CB00010B/1177